PERGAMON
(OXFORD)

Language Teaching Methodology Series

TEACHING ENGLISH
AS AN INTERNATIONAL LANGUAGE

From Practice to Principle

○

Other titles in this series include:

ALTMAN, Howard B and C Vaughan James *(eds.)*
Foreign language learning: meeting individual needs
BRUMFIT, Christopher J
Problems and principles in English teaching
CARROLL, Brendan J
Testing communicative performance
FREUDENSTEIN, Reinhold *(ed.)*
Teaching foreign languages to the very young
KELLERMAN, Marcelle
The forgotten third skill
LEONTIEV, Aleksei A
Psychology & the language learning process
NEWMARK, Peter
Approaches to translation
ROBINSON, Pauline C
ESP (English for specific purposes)
SHARP, Derrick W H
English at school: the wood and the trees

SYSTEM: *The International Journal of Educational Technology and Language Learning Systems (free specimen copies available on request)*

TEACHING ENGLISH
AS AN INTERNATIONAL LANGUAGE

From Practice to Principle

PETER STREVENS
Director of the Bell Educational Trust
and Fellow of Wolfson College, Cambridge

PERGAMON PRESS
Oxford · New York · Toronto · Sydney · Paris · Frankfurt

U.K.	Pergamon Press Ltd., Headington Hill Hall, Oxford OX3 0BW, England
U.S.A.	Pergamon Press Inc., Maxwell House, Fairview Park, Elmsford, New York 10523, U.S.A.
CANADA	Pergamon Press Canada Ltd., Suite 104, 150 Consumers Rd., Willowdale, Ontario M2J 1P9, Canada
AUSTRALIA	Pergamon Press (Aust.) Pty. Ltd., P.O. Box 544, Potts Point, N.S.W. 2011, Australia
FRANCE	Pergamon Press SARL, 24 rue des Ecoles, 75240 Paris, Cedex 05, France
FEDERAL REPUBLIC OF GERMANY	Pergamon Press GmbH, 6242 Kronberg-Taunus, Hammerweg 6, Federal Republic of Germany

First edition 1980
Reprinted 1982

British Library Cataloguing in Publication Data

Strevens, Peter, b. 1922
Teaching English as an international language.
- (Language teaching methodology series).
1. English language — Study and teaching
- Foreign students
I. Title II. Series
428'.2'407   PE1128.A2   80-40323
ISBN 0-08-025333-4

312590

6003/25590X

Printed in Great Britain by A. Wheaton & Co. Ltd., Exeter

Preface

My work involves me in some of the main areas of the learning and teaching of languages. In recent years I have been especially concerned with three central groups of issues: firstly, with efforts to understand better than previously the underlying nature of the language learning/language teaching process, the principal variables which determine the effectiveness of learning and teaching, and the ways in which different disciplines may contribute to this greater effectiveness; secondly, with the remarkable spread of English throughout the world, the proliferation of numbers of different yet related 'Englishes', their increasing function as a vehicle for the media of science or literature or administration, the emergence of unexpected roles for English in some overseas countries, and the consequences of all this for those who teach English as a foreign or second language; and thirdly, with 'scientific English' and the educational problems of those who learn and teach English for specific purposes, particularly for science and technology.

Most of the chapters of this book originated as papers delivered to conferences or seminars, though they have been considerably revised, mainly as a consequence of criticisms, comments, and debate at the time they were first aired. While the errors and exaggerations to be found in the book are my own responsibility, such enlightenment as it may contain is inspired by the great number of colleagues, students, and friends with whom I have been able to discuss these issues, as well as by the growing body of professional writings.

There is one further aspect of the contents of this book which I wish to underline, as I believe it to be of great importance: it concerns the long-standing tension between 'practice' and 'theory' in relation to language teaching. Throughout my career, when thinking about the practical experiences of teachers and hearing the perceptions of good teachers about how to make learning more effective, it has always seemed to me that these ideas have value at two different levels: *at their face value,* so that other teachers are enabled to do likewise (or to avoid doing likewise, as the case may be); but also *at a higher level of generality,* so that by generalizing from experience and across the perceptions of many teachers the profession may gain a deeper understanding of what it is doing, and may thereby acquire more power for effective action on a wider scale than that of the single individual teacher or learner.

In short, my concern has not been to say to teachers 'Your teaching should be done like this'—since they usually have greater practical experience than I have—but rather, to ask: What general principle underlies these experiences? or to seek similarities of pattern in other disciplines, in the hope that the experience and ideas of others may in some small degree assist our own efforts. Doing, it seems to me, is always helped by understanding.

In Part I all chapters display in one form or another this attempt to relate principle and practice. Chapter 1 looks at aspects of the *profession* of teaching languages; Chapter 2 considers the *learner,* the *teacher* and the *system* that brings them together, and asks what are the causes of failure in language learning and the conditions for success; Chapter 3 takes up the analysis of the many *variables* that influence achievement, particularly from the standpoint of the teacher; Chapter 4 illustrates the theme of 'practice' versus 'theory' by considering two different strands in English language studies: one which has been based on the pragmatic, descriptive study of the English language in its own terms, and another which derives directly from linguistic theory.

Part II deals with aspects of the global spread of English. In Chapter 5 there is a detailed discussion of the emergence of large numbers of localized forms of English (e.g. 'Indian English', West African English, Singapore English, etc.) and of their main features. Chapter 6 starts from the observation that English serves a greatly increased range of needs and purposes, and suggests that as a consequence of this enlarged scale of users and uses one must now distinguish two kinds of country: firstly, those where English is required for limited, conventional, *international* purposes, and secondly, those which now have major internal, *intranational* purposes for English. These latter countries (like India, Malaysia, Singapore, etc.) have become in a new sense 'English-using' countries, with large populations of their own citizens making use of localized forms of English for working and living. How are these localized forms of English to be viewed as educational targets? That is the question approached in Chapter 7. Chapter 8 describes the processes by which an international group of specialists first became aware of the international/intranational distinction and suggests that several lessons crucial for language teaching were learned as a by-product of coming to understand the distinction itself.

Part III is concerned with the use of English in relation to science. Chapter 9 contains a detailed survey of ESP (English for specific purposes) with a discussion of the advantages claimed for it and the prerequisites necessary to achieve these advantages. The chapter considers the relation of ESP to notional, functional, and communicative ideas, and to the developing principles of syllabus design. Chapter 10 is an analysis, on various planes, of 'scientific English' from the standpoint of teaching English as a foreign language. Finally, Chapter 11 discusses the special problems of the student, not a native speaker of English, who learns science through the medium of English.

In preparing the original papers and in making the revisions of them into book form I have been greatly helped by the patience and the professional skills of Miss E. M. Rice, Mrs. M. Moores, and Mrs. June Thompson, to whom I express my sincere thanks.

PETER STREVENS
Cambridge
January 1980

Acknowledgements

For permission to reprint in part or *in toto* papers previously published elsewhere, grateful acknowledgement is made to the following:

Part I

Chapter 1: Dr. Howard B. Altman and the American Council for the Teaching of Foreign Languages for permission to reprint an article which appeared in *Foreign Language Annals,* vol. 11, 1978.

Chapters 2 and 3: Dr. James Alatis and Teachers of English to Speakers of Other Languages for permission to reprint a paper published in *On TESOL '77* and part of a paper published in *On TESOL '79.*

Chapter 4: Oxford University Press for permission to print a revised version of a chapter from *In Honour of A. S. Hornby* (ed. Peter Strevens), 1978.

Part II

Chapter 5: The Culture Learning Institute, East-West Center, Hawaii, for permission to print a revised version of a paper published in *English for Cross-Cultural Communication* (ed. Larry E. Smith), 1980.

Chapter 6: The Department of Linguistics, University of Illinois, for permission to reprint a revised version of a paper published in B. Kachru (ed.) *(The) Other Tongue: English in Non-native Contexts,* Cambridge University Press, New York (forthcoming).

Chapter 7: The British Council for permission to print a revised version of a paper published in *ELT Documents: English as an International Language,* 1978.

Chapter 8: The Editor, *Indian Journal of Applied Linguistics,* for permission to reprint a revised version of a paper published in vol. 3, 1979.

Part III

Chapter 9:   Professor Braj Kachru for permission to reprint a paper given at a Seminar at the University of Illinois, Champaign-Urbana.

Chapter 10:   Dr. W. R. Lee and Oxford University Press for permission to reprint an article published in *English Language Teaching,* vol. 27, no. 3, June 1972.

Chapter 11:   The Editor of *Studies in Science Education* for permission to reprint a paper published in vol. 3, 1976.

Contents

PART I DEVELOPMENTS IN THE TEACHING AND LEARNING OF LANGUAGES

Chapter 1 Perspectives on the nature of learning and teaching languages   3

2 Causes of failure and conditions for success in the learning and teaching of foreign languages   18

3 Differences in teaching for different circumstances—or the teacher as a chameleon   29

4 'Practical' versus 'academic' in teaching English: the descriptive and the linguistic traditions   43

PART II PERSPECTIVES ON ENGLISH AS AN INTERNATIONAL LANGUAGE

Chapter 5 The expansion of English and the emergence of localized forms of English   61

6 International and intranational forms of English   79

7 When is a localized form of English a suitable model for teaching purposes?   84

8 English for international and intranational purposes: a shift in linguistic perspectives   91

PART III TEACHING ENGLISH FOR SCIENTIFIC AND OTHER SPECIFIC PURPOSES

Chapter 9 'Functional Englishes' (ESP)   105

10 Technical, technological, and scientific English (TTSE)   122

11 Problems of learning and teaching science through a foreign language   136

Bibliography   151

Index   161

Part I

DEVELOPMENTS IN THE TEACHING AND LEARNING OF LANGUAGES

Chapter 1
Perspectives on the Nature of Learning and Teaching Languages

This chapter is divided into three sections. Firstly, I shall try to indicate how our work brings together the concerns of the individual, of society, and of the language-teaching profession. Next I shall discuss some of the principal changes that cause severe problems for language teachers. Thirdly, I shall suggest that in responding to these changes and difficulties, we are in fact gaining a new understanding of our work. To back up this assertion I shall outline an overall view of the nature of the language learning/language teaching process.

I

The pupils and students we encounter in the classroom—whose learning we manage—remain with us only briefly before emerging into the world outside the classroom and beyond our immediate care. But the management of our students' learning during their time in our care is not simply a classroom task, and not simply a personal encounter between ourselves and other individuals, and not simply a brief sequence of contacts whose effect ceases when the students move out of our classroom and into the wider world outside. We teachers are inescapably a part of organized society: we have a social responsibility for ensuring that our students can cope with their life better in certain ways after our ministrations than they could before we met them. We must also recognize that our teaching efforts form part of two distinct time scales, each of which is far longer than our more familiar time scales of the semester, the year, or the course. Our students are developing human individuals, with a past before we meet them, a present while in our care, and a future after they leave us. They each have their own pace and programme of intellectual and social development, and what we do while they are with us ineluctably affects their

3

future attitudes and abilities as they metamorphose from the chrysalis of the student to the butterfly of the citizen.

To hold such a broad view of our professional task is to be, to some extent, an educator. It is indeed difficult to disentangle the technical procedures of classroom activity from the wider perspectives. Yet I believe that developments in our profession in the past 25 years enable us to distinguish three distinct though overlapping roles: those of the *instructor,* the *teacher,* and the *educator.* I am not, of course, referring to the academic grade or rank of 'instructor' which exists within a different universe of discourse. What I am trying to do is to suggest that within our work it is possible to identify these three general categories of pedagogical role, which are not mutually exclusive but illustrate complementary parts of the total task.

The *instructor* limits himself, deliberately or through immaturity, to presentation, to the techniques of instruction, to being an informant and not much more. He has few functions in organizing and planning the full programme of learning; he avoids responsibility (deliberately or incidentally) for the progress of individuals and classes throughout a long period of learning: he is concerned chiefly with technique and accuracy; he often has rather little professional training. The *teacher* is a good instructor, but more than an instructor; he is engaged in the deliberate management of learning and, therefore, with aims and goals and curricula and syllabuses and materials; with the main-tenance and improvement of professional standards for teachers; with keeping abreast of new ideas and methods not just in classroom terms but in relation to all the relevant disciplines; and with maximizing the learner's progress during his period of learning. The *educator* is a good teacher, but more than a teacher; he is also concerned with the relation, in terms of the learner, between language tuition and all the other elements in the student's curriculum; with the general social needs which his subject encounters and with how to meet other needs not yet adequately catered to by language teachers; with the function of education not simply for the individual, but within the wider population of one's own society and for mankind as a whole.

A major profession such as that of language teaching uses many instruments to regulate its activity and to disseminate its ideas, information, and attitudes. These include the formation of teachers' associations, the publication of journals, and the holding of conferences—whether these are solely concerned with principles and techniques, or designed more to boost the teachers' morale. All these activities, and others, form part of the career-long process whereby most of us begin our work as instructors, progress as a result of maturity and wisdom and experience to become not only instructors and teachers but educators as well. With very rare exceptions, it is impossible to be a true educator without being a good teacher, or to be a good teacher without being a competent instructor.

In other words, the three levels of pedagogue are in an inclusive relationship. And similarly for our pupils: this professional progression of ours mirrors the personal growth of the *student* into the *citizen*, and to that end all our instruction and teaching should serve the strategy of giving the learner not simply adequate classroom performance but, even more importantly, lifelong personal and civic competence.

II

Yet there is a deeper level of generality to be considered. Teachers must concern themselves with change and with our individual and collective professional responses to the truly awesome changes in society's demands upon us which we are currently living through. Some of the changes have come to affect the organized learning and teaching of languages in very many countries. They can be considered under these broad headings: changed social needs and educational functions of foreign languages, changed expectations and attitudes on the part of learners and students, and changes in approaches and methodology.

Changed social needs and educational functions of foreign languages
Foremost among these changes is the enormous growth of international communication. In almost every country in the world, far

more people are urgently required to have a much better command of more languages. This is an instrumental demand, not an intellectual or aesthetic one: people (and governments) need to understand and to respond and to act, in and through many languages. The change affecting us is a dual one, of *scale*—vastly increased numbers of people using languages—and also of *purpose*—no longer chiefly for the pursuit of literature and the humanities, but predominantly for instrumental use.

Some of those who (like myself) were trained in and for literary studies may lament the passing of the era when 'studying a foreign language' predominantly meant 'studying a foreign literature'. What society now demands is a predominance of practical command, given to a greater and more diverse population of language learners. There is still a place for the study of literature, but it is now a smaller place, relative to the total volume of language teaching; to retain even that diminished place, literary studies now have the unfamiliar and unwelcome task of justifying themselves. Of course, this is not to say that literature should not be studied. But it is necessary to point out the changed relationship of literary study on the one hand, and 'instrumental' courses on the other.

A second major change is away from languages as an offering for a limited élite (i.e. for the few learners destined for university studies) to languages for all (or nearly all). This change exerts two kinds of pressure upon us: firstly, we language teachers are unexpectedly faced with mixed-ability classes; secondly, we find that culturally oriented (and, especially, literary) courses turn out to be largely unsuitable for and unteachable to an unselected student population, at least in the conventional form of such courses. In general, we have not yet responded to this challenge by diversifying our teaching methods so that they can give equal help across the ability spectrum.

Thus, for example, the adoption of comprehensive education in Britain, Germany, and Scandinavia has caused severe difficulties of adjustment for language teachers, because it has replaced small classes of academically bright learners with large and often unstreamed classes. The problems created by this change are very difficult, and reaction to them has sometimes been feeble. Some people doubt whether the problems *can* be solved, and are beginning to advocate removing foreign languages from the school curriculum altogether. I do not share this point of view, because I believe that language teaching to school-age children *can* be reorganized in an acceptable and successful way. But this 'de-schooling' view is symptomatic of this change toward mixed-ability classes, and the fact that it can be seriously debated should make us realize how close our profession is to a serious organizational breakdown in some countries.

Linked with the expansion of language needs and with the extension from an élite to a nearly universal population of learners has come a change in the nature of courses for teaching languages to school-age children. The change is away from courses which are a pale reflection of conventional university studies—for example, by leading, without sufficient explanation or justification, to eventual concentration on literary works—toward courses which are designed to meet the needs of the school-age learner and to keep the learner interested, engaged, and even amused.

When this change began about 20 years ago, some teachers genuinely felt that their professional identity lay in the university studies by which they themselves had been trained, and they felt insecure and inadequate when asked to depart from the well-worn path. It is a measure of the growth in maturity of our profession that great numbers of teachers now find a new and a greater satisfaction in producing and teaching curricula, courses, and materials that relate more directly to the reality of our own pupils and their needs and possibilities, instead of being watered-down versions of conventional university courses.

Finally, we have to recognize the confusion that has been produced, notably in the United States but also elsewhere, through legal decisions requiring education to be provided in the mother tongue for members of various ethnic groups, both of immigrants and of indigenous communities. This is a trend whose consequences will continue to affect our profession, sometimes in quite unexpected ways, for some years ahead.

*Changed expectations and attitudes on the part of
learners and students*
Let us begin with an observation about differences between different
age groups. Young children everywhere still continue to learn
anything, including a practical command of foreign languages,
willingly and almost effortlessly. By contrast, adolescents and adults
expect to be given convincing reasons why they should learn, and if
they do not receive such reasons, if they do not perceive, and accept,
the relevance of a foreign language to their own lives, they are liable to
'turn off' their learning. Unwilling learners do not learn well or
easily—or at all! Yet, by a paradoxical extension of this same type of
change, *adult* learners increasingly realize that they need a practical
command of a language for their job or career and become eager and
effective learners, often through intensive courses for specific
purposes.

In short, at one end of the age scale, young children do not *seek*
relevance; at the other end, adults quickly *become aware* of it;
between the two, teenagers now *have to be convinced* of it by
argument and persuasion. If we are unable to convince them, we may
lose our teenage student population from language study while
gaining a vast, new, and specialized population of well-motivated
adults.

Other aspects of this type of change include the following: the focus of
classroom attention is less upon the teacher and teaching and more
upon the learner and his learning; participation and permissiveness
have affected, perhaps only temporarily, some of the methods that
students are willing to accept; with higher unemployment in America
and Europe, social prospects (i.e. Will I get a job?) colour our
students' attitudes toward learning; and so forth.

Changes in our approaches and methods
In recent years there has occurred a great and worldwide increase in
professionalism in language teaching. Teachers are better trained;
their average command of the language they teach continues to
improve (though there are still many lamentable exceptions to this
generalization); courses are increasingly designed to meet more precise

and specific needs of the learners; methods are more diverse and flexible and specialized, moving away from the aberration, above all, of believing that any single method could be the 'best' method in every teaching situation; our former excessive intellectual dependence upon and subservience to particular theoretical positions in linguistics and psychology has been replaced by the multidisciplinary approach of applied linguistics and the development of theoretical models of the language learning/teaching process in its own right.

III

This is perhaps the point at which we might turn from a catalogue of some of the principal changes in our profession to take up this question of studying the nature of the language learning/teaching process in its own terms, and to outline one possible way in which the enormous complexity and diversity of our profession can be reduced to order and simplicity.

Our task is in fact a simple one: we are attempting to identify the minimum elements of the language learning/teaching process, and to state how they affect each other. If we get it right, then *any* aspect of *any* language learning/teaching event can be accounted for somewhere in our statement, and the whole pattern ('model') should seem to make reasonable sense, at any rate as a first approximation.

The starting point for any comprehensive view of our subject is that it brings together a learner and teacher in a teaching/learning situation, and that this situation itself sets limits or constraints upon what is achieved. Contrary to the view held by many, I would insist that language teachers are only peripherally concerned with language *acquisition*. Even though some of the fundamental psychological strategies which operate in mother tongue acquisition undoubtedly also operate in foreign language learning—and work such as that of Corder and Selinker in studying interlanguage is therefore highly relevant to our profession—nevertheless, what we are doing entails so many complexities special to the organized teaching/learning situation that it requries to be analysed and stated in its own terms, which are not identical with those of psycholinguistics.

Where does the process start, and where does it end? Ultimately, it starts with society, with the 'public will' that language should be taught as part of the community's total educational offering; it ends with the individual learner, learning—or so we hope—the language he is being taught. Note that sometimes learning does not take place, for identifiable and systematic reasons, and these malfunctions should appear in the model, too. In other words, we are concerned not just with an ideal model of how languages ought to be taught and learned, but with a model of what actually happens, sometimes with success and sometimes with failure. We shall then find that a model of what happens *now* can still be useful in showing the way to greater effectiveness in the future.

The process ends with the learner. But the learner is in fact the justification for there being any organized language learning and teaching at all, so let us begin at the end, so to speak, with the ultimate element of the process, by outlining the contribution of the student, that is, the language learner, to the process.

The learner, it is essential to point out, is not simply a passive recipient of teaching, not just a walking Language Acquisition Device. On the contrary, the learner brings to the learning/teaching process a massive contribution of his own—an active and interactive personality, energized by a profile of varied qualities and abilities that shape the way in which he learns, and that therefore help to define the teaching which will be most effective and appropriate for him.

What kinds of qualities and abilities do we have to recognize? I believe that *all* learners share some basic potential for learning a foreign language, even though the eventual achievement in the language will be greater or less in different individuals. In other words, I do not believe in the existence of people who, although mentally and physically normal in all other respects, are unable to learn a foreign language. But individuals certainly do vary, in at least the following ways:

(1) in the extent to which they possess special abilities ('a good ear', powers of imitation and mimicry, or a superior verbal memory);

(2) in their previous experience of language (whether or not they are already literate in their own language, whether their language uses a writing system similar to that of the language they are learning, whether they have learned any other foreign language before—and if so, how many, in what relationship to the mother tongue, by what classroom methods, etc.);

(3) in their optimum personal learning rate, i.e. whether they are 'slow' or 'normal' or 'fast' learners (which varies at different points in their overall learning careers);

(4) in their preferred styles of learning and in the strategies of learning they develop (with or without the assistance of a teacher) at different times;

(5) in their learning stamina;

(6) in their requirements of praise, of encouragement, and of knowledge about their general standard of success;

(7) in their view of themselves as learners of languages;

(8) in their relations with teachers, which may either improve or impede their learning; and

(9) in their degree of willingness to learn, perhaps the most crucial of all, since the unwilling learner rarely learns.

All these variations, and no doubt others, are well known to teachers. The point is that the learner is neither passive nor stereotyped; the learner is an individual, and his individuality affects both his learning and the kind of teaching most likely to be effective for him at a particular moment.

The learner, then, is the ultimate element of the process we are studying. Let us now return to the origins of the process. Where do they lie, and what are the subsequent elements that lead on through the process until we reach, at the end of the line, the learner and his individual contribution to the process?

The process has its origins in 'the public will'—in the sociolinguistic situation. The languages systematically taught in a given country are a reflection of the wishes and expectations of society. Decisions to offer Russian or Chinese or Arabic, an increase or a decline in French or German or Italian, decisions to select and develop one particular language for national needs (as in Malaysia, Israel, or Tanzania) are obvious examples of the roots and origins of the language learning/teaching process. This is the first element of our model.

But the process has to be given substance. On the one hand, the organization and administration of education provides for teaching and teacher training, for salaries and pensions, for books and equipment, for courses and conferences. On the other hand, the learning and teaching of languages does not take place in a vacuum. Worldwide professions of education, of language teaching, and of allied disciplines exist together with a network of university and other centres of excellence and influence. This professional and disciplinary support is the place where practical experience and theoretical ideas flow in from other teachers and learners and scholars all over the world.

The answer to the question as to where linguistics comes into this model is, principally here, as one of a number of contributory disciplines. And if it should be objected that to show linguistics as merely one small part of one element out of many in the process is to give linguistics a low value, my reply is that this rather low status for theoretical linguists is probably appropriate, as contrasted with the overblown status it has been accorded in relation to language teaching in recent years. It is important not to be misunderstood: the position adopted here is absolutely not against linguistics as such. On the contrary, I would argue strongly in favour of the growing importance of linguistics in its own right. But two of the lessons we have learned in the past five years are these: (1) as linguistics becomes more theoretical, it becomes less directly relevant to language teaching; and (2) as language teaching becomes more sophisticated, we become better able to discover and understand the underlying principles and theories of its own nature—and that is another way of describing this search for a model of the language learning/teaching process.

To recapitulate thus far, the model has its origins in the public will, in sources of administration and finance, and in access to the worldwide storehouse of disciplinary and educational ideas and experience. Next, we must supply a number of closely related elements, all dealing with various aspects of the teacher and teaching.

The first of these is teacher training. It is here that the process makes use of the ideas and experience of the worldwide profession, is administered and financed according to the public will, and produces the appropriate number of teachers, suitably trained at an adequate standard, for the country's needs. There is a great deal that could be said about teacher training—about how it is usually fragmented and patchy, depending upon the energy and drive of a few individuals in influential positions; about suitable programmes of initial training and further training; about the deplorable absence, in most countries even now, of adequate national standards in the training of language teachers; etc. But for our purposes we need simply to note that a teacher training element is an essential component of any model of the total process.

The second of these elements concerned with teaching is the teacher, usually (but not always) the product of the preceding element. We shall skate rapidly past the details of this element, including the crucial questions of what constitute the minimum qualities of a teacher and of how language teachers can be helped to avoid the deterioration of their foreign language skills and encouraged to upgrade their professionalism. These are just some of the constituents of this element—the teacher—whose task, essentially, is the management of the pupil's learning.

The next element comprises a group of professional distinctions: approach, syllabus (US curriculum), methodology, and materials. Within this group of elements are to be found the ideologies, ideas, techniques, materials, and equipment we use in carrying out the 'teaching' part of the process. Briefly outlined, these elements are:

Approach is the fully developed 'package deal' of attitudes, principles, perhaps theories, backed by a substantial range of teaching materials and exemplifications of the ideology in practice that inform a particular school of thought in language teaching. Obvious examples are the Direct Method and the Audiolingual Method, both of which embodied a kind of ideology about the task.

Syllabus is the reasoned, principled statement of aims and objectives, of content, of sequence, of suggested methodology, of intensity and duration for a given course and for a given set of learners. This is an area in which great developments have been taking place in recent years, with new and additional principles of syllabus design following each other in rapid succession. Linguistic, situational, notional, functional, and communicative syllabuses: the complexity of syllabus design becomes ever greater. Hopefully, each new principle takes us nearer the aim of specifying more precisely the aims of the particular learners and the range of teaching programmes best suited to these particular aims.

Methodology means the entire gamut of teaching techniques, instructional procedures, and 'methods' (with a small 'm'). This is an area which is constantly expanding as teachers explore new and more effective ways of helping their learners to learn.

Materials refers to textbooks, readers, workbooks, flashcards, recordings, games, songs, reference books—all the vast range of pedagogical tools that teachers and learners make use of—together with the equipment and aids that may be necessary in order to present particular materials. A number of principles of materials design exist, some of which are similar to principles of syllabus design, though others are quite independent.

Now that our model of the language learning/teaching process has considered the elements relating to teacher training, the teacher, and the various components of teaching, one might think that it is nearly ready to be applied to the ultimate beneficiary, the learner. Before that happens, however, we must notice that there are some restrictions upon the learning/teaching process. Firstly, a given teaching/learning situation embodies a particular type of learning for which a particular type of teaching is best suited; secondly, a number of constraints have the effect of reducing, often very seriously, the success of learning and teaching.

Here we acknowledge that, for example, young children learn differently from adolescents or adults, and we therefore need to select different teaching techniques; similarly, the learning strategies of the beginner (at any age) are different from those of the intermediate or advanced learner, and we need to adjust our teaching accordingly. As a third example, the learning of a foreign language as part of a general education within the humanities, tending toward literary studies, entails a different kind of teaching from that which is appropriate if the educational framework is that of imparting a practical command of the language without deliberate reference to cultural features and different again from that which is required for 'specific-purpose' language teaching for occupational or educational use. These are a few of the factors which make it necessary for us to include an element dealing with the appropriate selection of learning/teaching types.

Other constraints and restrictions reduce the effectiveness of teaching and learning. Two types in particular are worth mentioning: (1) those which relate to quantity and intensity of instruction, and (2) what one might call physical and organization impediments. Sometimes the learner and the teacher find themselves required by authority to reach a particular target without being given enough time for learning and teaching. But much more important, perhaps, and very widespread, is the opposite situation in which a very small language content is taught over a very large number of hours. It is a serious possibility that the relatively poor achievement of school-age learners in many countries is principally due to dragging out a thin syllabus over several years. Another factor that almost certainly has a big effect is the intensity of teaching. Our profession lacks serious experimental evidence on this point, but the shared experience of teachers seems to be universally in favour of more intensive teaching, and to confirm that as intensity increases so also does the yield of learning per hour of teaching. The search for improvements in school-age language learning might well be helped by changing to shorter but more intensive courses—say, a maximum of 2 years' duration, but at not less than 8 - 10 hours per week.

Physical and organizational impediments to be considered include the obvious difficulties of fatigue, extreme heat or cold, noise, distraction, overcrowding, and so forth which have an effect on the degree of achievement of the learners, the teachers, and the educational system; we should also remember that almost all these constraints are man-made. They are very often simply the result of administrative decisions taken not by the teachers but by people who lack an understanding of their effect.

Now the picture is almost complete—except for mention of the fact that the process contains an evaluation system which works both formally and informally through the application of tests and examinations. We have now constructed a model which takes account of the public will; of administrative action and implementation; of the professional disciplines on which we rely; of teacher training, the teacher himself, and the various pedagogical components of our job; of the different types of learning and teaching; of the constraints of time and intensity, and of physical impediments; and, not least, of the subtle personal individuality of the learner, who constitutes, after all, the end and the justification for the entire process.

At this point we can begin to draw together the different strands of our argument. Language teaching in all countries operates within the same model which I have been outlining. And we can perhaps now understand also how changes in social needs and educational functions, changed expectations and attitudes on the part of the learners, and changes in approaches and methodology on the part of the teachers, all interact through this model.

In conclusion I wish to suggest that this relatively simple model can provide a first approximation to a blueprint for successful learning and teaching (that is the function of a model: to help organize one's thoughts in dealing with complex events). What are the truly crucial elements of the model? They would seem to be four:

(1) the learner—and he must be a willing learner;
(2) the teacher—who must have not only technical skill but also professional devotion to his learners;
(3) the community—which must provide the learners and teachers with the necessary moral and organizational support;
(4) the profession—which must supply the teacher with training, information, and support from all the contributing disciplines.

These four points lie behind the contention that: the greatest success in learning and teaching languages is typically produced when skilled and devoted teachers are encouraged, by society and their profession, to cherish willing learners.

This, I suggest, is the key to the link between the classroom and the world, to ways in which we can best help the student develop into the citizen, and to ways in which we teachers can exercise, with pride and satisfaction, our vital and civilizing function as educators.

Chapter 2

Causes of Failure and Conditions for Success in the Learning and Teaching of Foreign Languages

I. Introduction

A characteristic of the language-teaching profession is its enormous diversity and variability. Teachers of languages throughout the world are numbered in millions: learners of languages are counted in scores of millions. Hundreds of languages are involved, either as the target of learning or as the mother tongue of the learner. There are great numbers of different aims and objectives, different rates of intensity, different methods and materials and styles of learning, different levels of proficiency aimed at. And there is an equally wide range of results from total failure to learn to rapid and easy achievement.

Attempts in the past to overcome the variability of learners' achievement—i.e. to counter the lack of success of individuals or groups—have tended to concentrate on finding blanket solutions. We have justified our changes of direction by saying such things as: 'The method must be wrong'; or 'We need contrastive analysis'; or 'We ought to use language laboratories'; or 'We ought to stop using language laboratories'; or 'We must rely on linguistic theory'; or 'We must change our allegiance from one linguistic theory to another'; or 'We must change our classroom organization'; and so forth. Yet none of these changes brings about the overall improvement in learning that we assume it should produce, even though *some* improvement is often observed in *some* cases.

We must recognize that single, blanket solutions cannot be achieved. A close analysis of reasons for failure to learn, and of the conditions in which success is most often obtained, reminds us that while all human beings can be assumed to possess a universal potentiality for learning languages, their success in actually doing so in a framework of organized learning and teaching depends on very much more than this: it depends upon achieving the maximum harmony between a large number of variables, whose precise importance differs from one set of learning/teaching conditions to another.

We shall begin by briefly considering the nature of 'failure' and 'success', after which we shall suggest that a number of strong recurrent reasons for failure in language learning can be identified, as well as a number of strong recurrent conditions for success.

II. The meaning of 'failure' and 'success' in language learning

Used in a general way, the terms 'failure' and 'success' are imprecise and emotive; they gain significance by being related to specific aims. The more precisely we can state the targets of achievement for specific courses of learning and instruction, the more accuracy we can give to these terms 'failure' and 'success'. For the sake of argument, in what follows teaching is always assumed to have precisely specified aims and targets; what we are referring to is the extent to which these are attained in the time devoted to them. Furthermore, since 'failure' can be regarded as 'negative achievement' and 'success' as 'positive achievement', the term *achievement* is used henceforth as the general label.

There are, however, three different kinds of failure and success: the achievement of the *learner*, the achievement of the *teacher*, and the achievement of the *system* within which the learner and the teacher come together.

The achievement of the learner is the extent to which (a) he reaches his potential optimum rate of learning, and (b) he achieves control of the particular linguistic, functional, and communicative devices that make up the aims of his learning programme. Normally, language teachers have concentrated on the second of these subdivisions, i.e. on the learner's terminal command of the subset of the language he was seeking to learn. But in a deeper sense the learning/teaching process seeks (or should seek) not only to implant the terminal aims within the learner but also to activate his capacity to learn, and to do so at his *optimum learning rate,* i.e. at the fastest rate that he can sustain for the required period of learning.

The achievement of teachers is often measured by their record of examination passes among their pupils. This may be a convenient public index of pedagogical success, but in relation to the fundamental processes at work, examination passes are rather trivial. More importantly, the achievement of the teacher is the extent to which he or she achieves the *optimum management of learning.* To consider teaching as 'the management of learning' enables us to incorporate under a single concept both the learner's and the teacher's contribution to the learning process. This definition also enables us to accept any and every approach, method, and technique: 'the management of learning' is entirely non-specific as to methodology.

The achievement of the system is the extent to which it permits and even encourages the learner and teacher to reach their best rate of achievement in their respective roles. The 'system' includes (a) the sociolinguistic consensus—such factors as the popularity of a particular language, and the social status of learning and teaching languages, (b) the efficiency of the organization and administration of education, and (c) the particular school or other framework (including arrangments made for evaluation and assessment) within which the teacher and the learner come together.

Each of these three kinds of achievement has an indispensable role to play in the total learning/teaching process. Let us consider examples of each: an unwilling *learner* can cause failure in his own achievement in spite of a good teacher and a harmonious system, though equally an energetic and sophisticated learner can sometimes achieve success in spite of a poor teacher or a low-grade system; an incompetent *teacher* can prevent a learner from achieving success, but equally a good teacher may overcome learner-resistance or organizational faults in the system; a poor *system* can frustrate the efforts of learner and teacher alike (for instance, by allocating insufficient lesson time) but equally a well-designed system can often compensate for the less well-trained teachers or indifferent learners.

To summarize: success and failure can be re-stated as positive and negative achievement; they are best considered relative to specific aims; they relate in part to the learner, in part to the teacher, and in part to the system within which the learning and teaching occur.

Given this frame of reference for discussing achievement, two sets of circumstance can be identified, which are frequently associated either with failure or with success.

III. Strong recurrent reasons for failure

1. *Unwillingness to learn.* The attitude of the learner towards the task of learning spans a range from total unwillingness through passive neutrality to positive enthusiasm. There are many different reasons—personal, social, psychological, etc—for a learner's state of willingness, and a skilful teacher can often increase its extent. But the *un*willing learner usually fails to learn.

2. *Learner's expectations are too low.* Many learners, especially adolescents and adults, come to language classes convinced that they will not succeed. The reasons for a negative self-view are many, and often they can be modified or changed into high expectations by a skilful teacher; but low expectations are a serious impediment. Examples: (i) A university student whose course required her to learn Spanish informed us that she was unable to learn languages. In spite of patient and caring teachers, her view of herself remained inviolate for several months: she learned virtually no Spanish. Then suddenly, after about 5 months, she started to make good progress. But she found it so difficult to accept this falsification of her predictions about herself that she preferred to withdraw from the course rather than go on learning Spanish. (ii) A major French oil-tanker company is sometimes required to send a captain to take over a ship with an English-speaking crew at short notice. Courses of up to 100 hours are arranged, but these non-academic learners do not believe that they can 'learn English' in that time, so they begin the course with expectations of total lack of success.

Except in extreme cases, the learners' expectations of their own success are based very closely on the opinions expressed by their teachers.

It is therefore possible by careless talk to blight the achievement of a learner; equally it is possible by encouragement to bring about considerable improvement.

3. *Unrealistic aims.* These are generally a fault of the system rather than of the learner or the teacher, e.g. the commercial language school that advertises 'You can speak English in 24 hours'. But many school language programmes make presumptions about the learners' terminal achievements which, as teachers themselves often acknowledge, cannot in fact be reached by the average pupil. The learners generally know this—students are very sensitive about such matters—and thus unrealistic statements of aims on the part of the teacher or the system trigger low expectations on the part of the learner, thereby turning them into self-fulfilling prophecies.

4. *Off-set teaching.* This is a special case of unrealistic aims. It occurs, not infrequently, when what the learners are expected to *learn* is the language, but what the teachers are required to *teach* is something different. Three examples are (i) when *literature* is taught in the belief that this will thereby teach the language but before the learners have the necessary command of language to follow and understand; (ii) when *linguistics* is taught as a substitute for teaching a command of the language; (iii) when a largely oral English course is required to be taught by teachers who have no effective command of the spoken language.

5. *Physical and organizational impediments.* Obvious examples are: *fatigue, heat* or *cold, noise* or *distraction.* Weary learners learn little; weary teachers teach little. Great heat or cold or other physical discomforts reduce the rate of learning; excessive noise, whether from other classes, or city traffic, or monsoon rain drumming on corrugated iron roofs, makes language learning nearly impossible; the classroom which overlooks a swimming pool, or is the constant target for the Principal's visitors, distracts the learners. Other examples include *overcrowding, lack of premises, books, or equipment, examination neurosis, absenteeism* on the part of the learner or the teacher.

It is essential to note that all these impediments are ultimately avoidable. Unfortunately teachers are inclined to accept such impediments as acts of God, as features of the universe which are to be borne with fortitude but are not susceptible of improvement by human effort. But they are nearly always the man-made consequences of poor organization or educational policy. In some ways language teachers are more inclined than others to put up with these impediments. Our colleagues who teach science, or woodwork, or other crafts, do not tolerate conditions in which they are prevented from teaching their subject: and neither should we. Very often these difficulties are tolerated for far too long by teachers who fail to realize that it is an essential part of a teacher's duty to campaign, individually and collectively, for the removal of such impediments. The campaign may take a very long time, but it should never be abandoned. In these matters the teachers know best: it is essential to their professional integrity that they should not acquiesce, except temporarily, in the continuance of physical and organizational impediments to learning and teaching.

6. *Insufficient time for learning and teaching.* This deficiency relates to the *total quantity* of time for organized instruction and its rate of intensity as well as the overall duration of courses. Some courses, particularly 'service' language courses—'English for engineering students', for example—are allocated by course administrators ludicrously few total hours of instruction. Or courses are persistently taught so thinly, say 3 or 4 hours per week, that learning is almost guaranteed to be equally thin and inadequate. At the other extreme, some courses with a rather small syllabus content are taught over periods of 6, 8, even 10 years: teachers are usually well aware that after the first 2 years of school instruction in a language there is a strong tendency for standards to decline, not to improve, with all its consequent disillusion and frustration for teachers and learners alike.

7. *Gross incompetence in teaching.* Although standards of entry to teaching are improving, and standards of teacher training are improving even more rapidly, there still exist numbers of language teachers whose management of their pupils' learning remains incompetent. The teacher whose personality 'turns off' the learners; the teacher

with an inadequate command of the foreign language; the teacher without the necessary instructional techniques—these are some of the most obvious examples. These are defects of the teacher, but also of the educational system that tolerates them, and the teaching profession should continue to campaign for their eradication.

8. *When the teachers/materials equation is not solved.* The higher the general standard of the teachers, the less important are the course-books and other teaching materials. But when the standard of teachers is low, as it inevitably is for a time in conditions of rapid expansion of education, then the standard of teaching materials assumes great importance. This is what is meant by 'the teachers/materials equation'. Insufficiently trained teachers working with poor materials face a considerable handicap. When this occurs it is a defect of the system, for whose remedy a three-way collaboration is necessary between publishers, administrators, and teachers.

9. *Teachers inadequately prepared.* As the standards of initial teacher training continue to rise worldwide, the crux of this problem falls increasingly upon the older teachers who may not have profited from present-day standards. The problem is especially acute when a major change takes place in approach or methodology which the teachers who are products of earlier stages of development may not be aware of or may not accept. An example of this has recently occurred in Britain, where the introduction of French in the *primary* school has faced severe difficulties in some areas because of the unwillingness of some *secondary* school teachers to adjust to the change in their intake of pupils. Here it is the system which may need to persuade and re-educate the teachers in order to permit the continued achievement of the learners.

These, then, seem to me to be the most frequent strong recurrent reasons for failure. All of them are avoidable, though some require major changes of administrative policy. Now let us turn to strong recurrent reasons for success, i.e. conditions that seem regularly to be associated with higher levels of achievement.

IV. Strong recurrent reasons for success

1. *Willing learners.* Enthusiasm for learning is a great asset and one which teachers can nurture in their learners. Most individuals vary from time to time in their degree of willingness, often as a result of emotional ups and downs in their home life. It is a central component of good teaching that the teacher should be aware of these changes, sympathetic to their underlying causes, and continually seeking to cajole and encourage the learner upwards to his optimum willingness to learn.

2. *Learners see the relevance of their learning.* It is only for a fairly short period in childhood that human beings willingly learn without caring why they should do so. It may be that one of the inherent difficulties in school language learning is that as they approach adolescence children cease to learn insouciantly, without caring or knowing why, and start to expect clear and valid reasons for continuing to give their willingness to learn a language. Rates of achievement are greatly improved when learners know and accept the reasons for learning.

3. *Learners' expectations are high.* A belief that one *will* learn is a powerful incentive to actually do so.

4. *The target language has good standing in the community.* It is a sociolinguistic truism that learning and teaching an unpopular language is a difficult task. By contrast, when the foreign language has a high status or is taken for granted, achievement tends to be high. (This is a variable over which the teacher has little control, as learners' attitudes tend to be established before they start to learn, along the lines of current popular opinion and prejudice.)

5. *Physical and organizational requirements are met.* Two different types of provision have to be considered. The first relates to the absence of the impediments noted earlier: fatigue, extremes of temperature, etc. The second concerns the actual provision and the efficient working of all necessary buildings, plant, equipment, and aids. There are countries where the slow construction of school buildings creates huge classes, where textbooks are prescribed and imported but

are not actually received by the teachers or the pupils, where tape recordings or language laboratories exist but have long since irretrievably broken down for lack of skilled technicians, where overhead projectors have been supplied but cannot be used because it is too costly to replace lamp bulbs, where even blackboards are almost illegible through old age and desuetude. Although such shortcomings are trivial they deeply affect the morale of the teachers and hence affect the learning prospects of the learners. But where the educational system is well ordered, well provided, and efficiently maintained, learning rates tend to be high—all else being equal.

6. *Realistic aims accepted by all.* It is self-evident that the establishment of aims that are realistic should improve the climate of learning and teaching. But it is also necessary to state that these aims should be known to and accepted by the teachers as a whole and enlightened public opinion in addition. Otherwise one is preparing the way for failures such as those mentioned in relation to some areas of primary school French in England.

7. *Suitable syllabuses.* The syllabus is potentially the most important single pedagogical formulation to bear upon any learning/teaching situation. We might define the ideal syllabus as a statement of *aims, approach, content, sequence,* and *preferred methodology* for a given set of learners and teachers. With so many elements to be incorporated within a single formulation there are many opportunities for inadequacy. Yet our understanding of the principles of syllabus design has recently been revised, extended, and modernized in ways that now make it possible to provide, for any course in learning and teaching languages, a formulation of great potential benefit. When this is done it can be a major source of guidance and support for the teacher and, through the teacher, a major influence upon the learner's progress and achievement and a head start towards higher rates of achievement.

8. *Intensity of teaching relatively high.* Although virtually no research has been carried on the subject, there is a widespread belief among teachers who have tried it that an increase in the intensity of teaching leads to a more than proportionate increase in the rate of learning per

unit time. There seems to be a lower limit of around 5 or 6 hours per week, below which the learning yield per hours drops off drastically. The range of intensity from this 5-hour point up to another and rather different borderline, at around 20 hour per week, seems to constitute what one might call the normal range of intensity. 'Normal' here means that few alterations of method are required because of increases in intensity: above 20 hours per week there is some experience that special precautions need to be brought in to guard against fatigue, boredom, too-long contact with the same teacher, and other technical difficulties. If the necessary precautions *are* taken, successful learning at intensities up to 40 or 50 hours per week, sometimes even beyond, have been reported. Within the 'normal' range of 5-20 hours per week it is widely accepted that the learning yield per hour increases directly with intensity, i.e. more learning takes place in 20 hours of instruction when it takes place in one single week than in 20 hours when they are spread over 4 weeks. Perhaps part of the reason for this is that the lower rate of intensity includes 4 weeks of opportunities for forgetting. The assertion being made here is that rates of achievement are improved by higher rates of intensity in teaching and learning.

9. *Teachers have a high level of professional competence.* If we consider the full range of professional training as a language teacher it is beginning to look as if a quantum jump in effectiveness in the management of learning takes place at a particular point—a point which relatively few teachers have reached until recently but which is becoming increasingly common. In Britain, at least, this watershed point is generally associated with an opportunity for intensive *further* professional training following some 7-10 years of experience (e.g. typically in a 1 year master's course in applied linguistics or TEFL/TESL). Some rare, gifted teachers achieve this out of their own personal resources. By whatever means, it seems that a process of in-service professional maturation slowly takes place in the mind and understanding of the practising teacher, at the end of which the opportunity for some months of intensive thinking, reading, and discussion produces a fresh burst of competence, confidence, and morale.

This applies to teachers from any country; teachers who have achieved this professional regeneration become exceptionally well able to maximize the progress of their learners.

10. *Teachers cherish learners.* The verb *to cherish* appears very rarely in the literature of language learning and teaching. Its use here implies that the best teachers *know* their pupils, *encourage* them, *show concern* for them, *find out their interests, discover their learning preferences, monitor their progress with a sympathetic eye, unravel their difficulties—cherish them* as human beings engaged in a collaboration of learning. There is a rough analogy here with 'intensive care' in hospitals, where the patient is constantly watched by skilled professional people whose first concern is to help the patient to want to live. We are concerned not only with helping our learners to learn, but with ensuring that even when they experience great difficulties they still *want* to learn.

Of all the strong recurrent reasons for success, this last is the most important and the most effective, and when it occurs it is frequently associated with the high level of professionalism referred to above, since it is normally teachers at this level who are not only best able to sense the learner's immediate needs but also have the broad range of professional skills to enable them to compensate in some degree for defects elsewhere in the total learning/teaching situation.

V. Conclusion

The conception of failure and success in language learning outlined in this chapter is based upon the notion of the whole and individual learner, not just upon the universal but common characteristic of language acquisition. The various factors touched on in this chapter can be summarized in a single aphoristic sentence:

> *Maximum rates of achievement in the learning and teaching of a foreign language are typically produced when skilled and devoted teachers are encouraged by society and their profession to cherish willing learners.*

Chapter 3

Differences in Teaching for Different Circumstances—or the Teacher as a Chameleon

The two previous chapters have been concerned, respectively, with the wider scope of the profession of language teaching and with those variable elements in the learning/teaching situation that are commonly associated with greater failure or success. This third chapter addresses itself to the effect on the teacher and on his teaching of certain important features. Its basic hypothesis is, that to be effective in promoting learning, teaching must take account of and respond to a large number of variables. The topic will be divided into three sections: first, the way in which our professional perceptions of the variables in language teaching have changed over the years; second, an analysis of the variables that seem to operate; and, third, some consequences of these changing perceptions and these variables.

I. Our changing perceptions of the variables

Very few of us see more than a small selection of the main variables—just those variables, in fact, which operate with obvious effect in our own particular circumstances. What is more, even if all teachers agreed in their understanding of those variables they could observe and identify—which they do not—it is only by pooling and comparing their observations and their responses that we gradually establish a full perspective of the complex activity we are all engaged in.

In this regard we have been, in the past 20 years, somewhat in the position of those Blind Men of Indostan in the poem by John Godfrey Saxe (an American poet of the early nineteenth century) who encountered an elephant for the first time.

The Blind Men and the Elephant (A Hindoo Fable)

It was six men of Indostan
  To learning much inclined,
Who went to see the Elephant
  (Though all of them were blind).
That each by observation
  Might satisfy his mind.

The *First* approached the Elephant,
  And happening to fall
Against his broad and sturdy side,
  At once began to bawl:
'God bless me! but the Elephant
  Is very like a wall!'

The *Second,* feeling of the tusk,
  Cried, 'Ho! what have we here
So very round and smooth and sharp?
  To me 'tis mighty clear
This wonder of an Elephant
  Is very like a spear!'

The *Third* approached the animal,
  and happening to take
The squirming trunk within his hands,
  Thus boldly up and spake:
'I see,' quoth he, 'the Elephant
  Is very like a snake!'

The *Fourth* reached out an eager hand,
  and felt about the knee.
'What most this wondrous beast is like
  Is might plain,' quoth he;
' 'Tis clear enough the Elephant
  Is very like a tree!'

The *Fifth,* who chanced to touch the ear,
  Said: 'E'en the blindest man
Can tell what this resembles most;
  Deny the fact who can,
This marvel of an Elephant
  Is very like a fan!'

The *Sixth* no sooner had begun
  About the beast to grope,
Then, seizing on the swinging tail
  That fell within his scope,
I see,' quoth he, 'the Elephant
  Is very like a rope!'

And so these men of Indostan
  Disputed loud and long,
Each in his own opinion
  Exceeding stiff and strong,
Though each was partly in the right,
  And all were in the wrong!

MORAL:

So oft in theologic wars,
  The disputants, I ween,
Rail on in utter ignorance
  Of what each other mean,
And prate about an Elephant
  Not one of them has seen!

(JOHN GODFREY SAXE, 1816-87)

We, perhaps, are in a happier position than Saxe's wise men, because our 'elephant' has been reported, observed, photographed, and subjected to minute analysis and discussion for the past dozen years. As a result we share a more comprehensive and accurate understanding of what an elephant is like than Saxe's blind Indostanis could muster—though at the same time we are increasingly aware that there is not just one elephant but whole families and populations and even subspecies of elephants, and that therefore the scope of our study gets ever wider, even as our comprehension of it grows.

You will recall that one reason for the complementary analyses given by Saxe's blind men was that they each observed the elephant from a different standpoint. It is interesting to notice that a whole sequence of different viewpoints about the nature of our own profession, TESOL, is embodied in the sequence of acronyms or initials that have been employed on both sides of the Atlantic. The proto-TEFL term, as it were, was probably ELT (English language teaching), the original undifferentiated term used in Britain as early as 1945 and still employed today, e.g. in the title of the British *ELT Journal,* founded in 1948. Before long it became necessary, especially in British ELT, to distinguish between ELT in circumstances where the language had a special historical status in the community, for instance English in Nigeria, or Hong Kong, or Fiji (where it is referred to as a *second* language, hence ESL), and, on the other hand, ELT in circumstances where the language has no special standing and is not in widespread use, i.e. where it is a *foreign* language, as in Japan or Brazil: hence EFL. In British usage, when referring to the teaching of English to foreign students visiting Britain, the term TEFL became universal because such students almost always come from and return to 'foreign language' countries. To sum up the distinction, for us in Britain ESL indicates sociolinguistic conditions in a foreign country which compel significant changes in teaching English there.

In the United States, though, I sense a great deal of free variation, uncertainty, even change of meaning, in the use of the terms TEFL and TESL. For a given activity, sometimes the one is used and sometimes the other. There are, perhaps, two reasons for this: first, the American profession has been relatively little engaged in ESL in the British sense (i.e. in former British countries) so that this EFL/ESL distinction has had little relevance; but in addition the issue has been clouded by multiple meanings for the word 'second'. By talking of a 'second language'—meaning the next one learned after the mother tongue—and by talking of a 'second *foreign* language' (or a third, or fourth)—e.g. Spanish, French, German, etc., in the school system—we have encouraged semantic ambiguity. By contrast, the name of the teachers' organization, TESOL, is clear and unambiguous in the way it unites *all* branches of the profession.

What terms came next? There is some uncertainty about the chronology. My own understanding is that the next development occurred when the special and contentious problem arose of teaching English to children of the black community in the United States: was it to be regarded as 'mother-tongue' teaching? Should it be handled as a branch of TEFL? Black English became accepted as a dialect of English to be reckoned with in educational terms, and in this way ESOD or TESOD were born—and even ESOLD and TESOLD: teaching English to speakers of other languages and dialects.

Yet that is not by any means the end of these subdivisions within our own profession. The term ESP (English for specific purposes) has come into universal use to designate the teaching of English not in general, but with particular restrictions on its aims, content, or skill objectives. And within ESP, EST refers to English for science and technology, a particular subset of ESP, which entails special learning features (and special teaching requirements, too) since the scientist or engineer has to learn 'the language of science'—whatever that is. The British Council favours a further internal distinction within ESP: EAP (English for *academic* purposes) and EOP (for *occupational* purposes).

There have been other TEFL terms: EIAL (English as an international auxiliary language) had a brief existence in Hawaii before being dropped in favour of an INTER/INTRA distinction (English for *inter*national purposes, as in Japan, Brazil, etc., and English for *intra*national purposes, as for large populations of people in India, Malaysia, and Singapore, and increasingly in other historically English-using countries.)[1]

Two other terms now in constant use have not been turned into acronyms or initials. In the United States, 'bilingual education' is a specialized and established branch of English teaching, while in Britain we refer to 'immigrant teaching', which is that special branch of teaching English to the children of immigrants within the framework

[1]See particularly Smith (1980) and chapters 6 to 9 of this book.

of the ordinary State school system—in fact, as a sort of TEFL-flavoured mother-tongue programme.

The lesson to be learned from this sequence of TEFL terms is that in the short space of 25 years our perceptions of some major variables within our own profession have repeatedly grown sharper and more delicately differentiated, so that our existing ways of referring to what we do have become inadequate, and have required the development and acceptance of a dozen or more specialized terms. And there will undoubtedly be more distinctions made in the future.

Yet the terms we have discussed above are only macro-variables, as it were. Beyond these macro-variables are a whole range of other choices, distinctions, alternatives, divergences—and the operation of these variables affects our daily professional activity.

II. An analysis of the variables[1]

When we attempt a reasonably comprehensive survey of the many variables which in total affect our profession, some teachers will already be aware of all the factors I shall mention, and more. Others, especially teachers who have always worked in one particular branch of TEFL, will be like Saxe's *Blind Men of Indostan* because they will have seen some of the variables in action while being unaware, perhaps, of others, teachers with different experience will recognize a different selection, depending on which part of the TEFL elephant's anatomy they have been concerned with.

TEFL teachers who move from one kind of teaching to another—from teaching 'general' TEFL to adults in the United States or Britain, to teaching children in Colombia, to teaching intensive ESP for medical staff in a country on the Arabian Gulf, to university TEFL in Scandinavia, to teacher training in Singapore—such peripatetic teachers quickly discover that there are, indeed, a great many variables at work. Let us look at five types:

[1] The identification of variables has a long history. The analysis in this chapter is concerned more with emphasizing the scope and diversity of types of variables rather than with comprehensivity in detail. It builds on the work of very many specialists (see References). But one work above should be singled out for its subtlety and wide coverage of variables in the learning and teaching of languages, i.e. Wm. F. Mackey's (1965) *Language Teaching Analysis*.

1. *Some variables appear as restrictions upon what the teachers are actually permitted to do:* e.g. in cultural matters. In some societies, for instance, the kind of boy-girl relationships commonly found in TEFL textbooks, illustrations of girls in short dresses, reference to alcoholic drinks, mention of dogs as domestic pets, even relaxed relations between teachers and students if they are of different sexes—all these may be culturally unacceptable.

2. *Other variables will appear as limits on what is physically and organizationally possible:* very large classes; classroom furniture bolted to the floor (which severely restricts communicative activity and work in groups); inadequate numbers of classes per week; a school year that is nominally of 30 teaching weeks but in practice may be of 20 weeks or less; lack of central authority—or alternatively such draconian central authority that any deviation from normal practice, even creative experiment by intelligent teachers, becomes almost a criminal offence; absence of suitable textbooks, teaching aids, or equipment, even of blackboards and exercise books.

3. Some variables will affect the teacher through *general levels of teacher training,* where the national average level of professional competence has pervasive consequences on what can be achieved in the classroom.

4. Yet other variables relate to *sociolinguistic attitudes and expectations:* if English is an unpopular language in a given place (for instance, in rural Quebec at present), teaching it may be ineffective for the learner and unpleasant for the teacher; if a community normally expects that its citizens *will* learn English (e.g. in Holland or Scandinavia) they generally do so, but conversely, low expectations (as of learning foreign languages by English school children) are fulfilled by generally poor standards of achievement.

5. *The educational framework* of TEFL, too, may vary: in some places the teaching of English begins at age 7 or 8 and continues as a part of normal, liberal arts education, for up to 10 or 11 years; elsewhere it starts only at age 14 and lasts for 4 years (and for some students their long years of English in school may seem irrelevant

and be largely ineffective); by contrast, the framework for ESP is almost always that of adult education: it is often independent of the rigid administrative matrix of general education, and is usually open for methodological originality, i.e. ESP is not tied to any particular method or materials, and in consequence the successes and failures in ESP are more directly caused by the teachers, as distinct from the system, than is the case in a general educational framework, where the system often casts the variables into a mould which makes success difficult to achieve save by exceptional teachers.

Five sets of variables have been mentioned so far: restrictions on teaching, physical and organizational constraints, standards of teacher training, sociolinguistic attitudes, the educational framework. They can all be roughly classified as derived from *the community,* that is to say, from the mixture of sociolinguistic conditions and the current realities of educational administration. Teachers in Britain or America or Australia are, of course, equally subject to constraints of this type, but in those countries teachers tend to be unaware of them and only realize their existence on first working abroad, or occasionally at home when some really major reform is being fought through our various pieces of legislative and administrative machinery.

From variables ascribable to *the community,* and generally acting as constraints on the teacher, let us turn to other variables more directly under the control of teachers, or at least of *the teaching profession* at large. It is necessary to do this in order to remind ourselves that although teachers work to a large extent within a matrix of conditions that are not of their choosing and are only minimally under their control, nevertheless in addition teachers themselves do have the responsibility for selecting among a wide range of further variables.

The most obvious sets of teacher-controlled variables fall under the twin headings of *syllabus* and *methodology,* i.e. the large and growing range of instructional techiques available to the teacher (roughly 'methodology') and the principles for selecting and organizing the content to be taught (broadly, 'syllabus design').

The two are inter-linked. Modern views about the importance of the learner lead us to analyse the learner's needs in ever-greater detail, to establish with maximum certainty his precise aims and objectives; then to specify the language and other content he will require and to organize the sequence in which it is most appropriate to teach this content to this learner; and also to consider what teaching techniques can most effectively be used by the teachers available to teach *this* content in *this* sequence to *these* learners with these needs.

The first two parts of that process—analysing the learner's needs and objectives, and determining appropriate content and sequence—form part of *syllabus design.* This is a process where members of the teaching profession consider several dimensions in order to establish the best possible 'fit' or matching. What are these dimensions? Here are some of them. The identity of the learners and their principal characteristics (age, educational level, stage of proficiency already reached, etc.); their aims and objectives (to pass a particular examination, to achieve practical oral communication with certain types of people, to read with understanding certain kinds of written text, etc.); the language appropriate to those objectives (which may either be 'general English' or may be some defined subset of English, like 'English for Indian village tropical health projects', or 'English for air traffic control', etc.); whether there is any special need for some items to be taught before other items (e.g. in an ESP course for ships' officers to teach compass directions and bearings early on, where in contrast they might be taught later—or never—in a course for specialists in tropical medicine): these are some of the dimensions to be considered.

In considering them, the syllabus designer will bear in mind several different aspects of the content: linguistic, situational, notional, functional, and communicative. *Linguistic* aspects, i.e. the language content to be learned in terms of grammar, vocabulary, pronunciation, formulae and fixed expressions, idioms, and so forth. *Situational* aspects: how to make the language content more interesting, more easily learned and remembered, and more like real life, by teaching it in relation to familiar or imaginative situations, like 'at the Post Office', 'telling the time', 'going to school', and so forth. *Notional* aspects: ways in which various fundamental notions about the universe are expressed in English—notions of time, of place, even of case (i.e. 'who does what, who to, and with what result'). *Functional* aspects: how English expresses certain functions of language, such as negation, possibility and impossibility, description, questioning, judgements, and many others. *Communicative* aspects: how to use English for meaningful, deliberate, effective communication between human beings, including discoursal and rhetorical rules.

Methodology, too, is a variable whose manipulation is normally open to the teacher, not imposed upon him or her by outside authority. The term includes both 'strategic' and 'tactical' decisions. Strategic decisions include such questions as: the balance of importance and time to be given to the various 'skills' of speaking, reading etc.; the extent to which overt use is made of grammar, and what kind of grammar it will be; the extent of individualized procedures, if any; the relation between the teaching syllabus and any terminal assessment or examination; the degree of reliance upon class work and private study; the use or otherwise of language laboratories and other aids; and similar choices, and many others. 'Tactical' decisions include: the selection of particular teaching techniques at particular points in each course and each lesson, the flexibility of teachers to change their techniques from moment to moment according to the learning paths of the students, the encouragement of methodological originality and creativity on the part of the teacher (and even the learner, on occasion), and many more choices of this limited kind.

Compared with the central importance of syllabus design and methodology, the variables of *materials production* and *evaluation* are perhaps secondary, even though their impact on the daily classroom life of the teacher and the learner is often considerable. There is, however, one further variable on the 'teaching' side (as distinct from the 'community' side), which must not be overlooked: *teacher training.* To the individual teacher, teacher training is usually looked at in terms of preparation for his or her personal career. The individual learner rarely even considers the question except perhaps to reassure himself that he is being helped to learn by someone who is at least not an amateur—much as the patient awaiting surgical treatment likes to be certain that he is not in the hands of a do-it-yourself hobbyist. Yet on a larger scale the extent, nature, and quality of the teacher training available in a given country will crucially affect the quality of teaching that is normally given there; and it will also largely determine which choices are made under the variables of syllabus design and methodology. So when we observe different kinds of teaching and different standards of teaching taking place under different conditions we can be sure that the kind of teacher training undergone by the teacher will be a major determiner thereof; and we can also be certain that if we are seeking ways of modifying the teaching and learning in a given place, we shall be bound to include the teacher-training system in our calculations.

The variable of *teacher training* embraces many elements. If one accepts that teachers are by definition members of the educated sector of the community (and that the notion of an uneducated teacher is, or ought to be, a logical contradiction), then a prime element in teacher training concerns the level of personal education possessed by the trainee teacher. A case can be made for the view that teaching, being a matter of close and continuous interaction between individual human personalities, also requires a high level of emotional maturity and stability. Then one must consider the balance between the three main components of a teacher-training course: a *skills* component, which develops practical, instructional techniques, both those common to all branches of teaching and those that are special to TEFL—including, incidentally, an adequate command of the language he or she is teaching; an *information* component, in which the teacher takes in the very considerable body of knowledge about education, teaching, language, English today, sociology, psychology, the organizational framework he is working in, and much more; and in addition a *theory* component, which provides him with an intellectual basis for knowing not just *what* to teach and *how* to teach it, but also *why* to teach that rather than something else. Let us consider, in passing, just one example of the kind of information that ought to be included in TEFL training courses. It concerns the astonishing changes that are taking place in the spread and functions of English on a global scale. Young teachers need to be informed about the way that English is now widely regarded abroad as an international possession—it is no longer the cultural property of the British, the Americans, the Australians, and the New Zealanders. Teachers need to realize that in a growing number of countries, e.g. India, Singapore, parts of Africa, English is used by vast and growing populations of people (26 millions in India alone) who never meet native speakers of English and who have no desire or need to model their English on ours. We have to get rid of our monolingual ethnocentricity and accept the existence of a great many localized forms of English, one characteristic of which is precisely that they are *different from* British and Australian and American English. There are many other kinds of information to be included: this may serve simply as an example.

We must now look briefly at one other set of variables that affect our teaching: variables relating to the *learner*. To list them all would be a major task: we now recognize that TEFL learners are human beings (as distinct from laboratory animals) and that while they share certain universal human characteristics they also each carry a wide range of strictly individual features. How can we distinguish those that are significant from among the mass of learner characteristics?

There are three learner variables above all, it seems to me, which lie at the heart of the interaction between learner and teacher and determine how effectively the learner learns. There are: (1) the learner's *reasons for learning*; (ii) his or her *attitudes towards learning*; and (iii) his or her *expectations of learning*.[1]

Learners' *reasons* for TEFL learning vary very greatly: for young children they are simply that it is normal and enjoyable to do what teacher says; for adolescents they are often founded on hazy notions of 'relevance' and on emotions of love or hate towards the teacher, and they are frequently negative reasons, so that learning does not occur; for adults, the reasons are generally quite definite and instrumental.

---

[1] I am deliberately avoiding the term *motivation*, partly because it has different meanings for different people, but chiefly because *motivation* embraces a large number of factors. The three-term analysis into *reasons, attitudes,* and *expectations* is made from the standpoint of the teacher rather than on a basis of psychological or sociological analysis.

Learners' *attitudes* towards TEFL learning are a compound of their attitudes towards learning in general, towards English in particular, towards the teacher and the textbook, even towards themselves as learners.

Learners' *expectations* of TEFL learning are based partly on their past history and experience of language learning, partly on opinions fed to them by their family, their friends, and their teacher, and partly on the current folk-myth about whether his community normally expects people to learn English.

As far as teachers are concerned, they quickly discover two things: first, that the success of their own efforts in the management of learning and of their learners' efforts in achieving their optimum learning rate (Strevens, 1977) depends heavily on these reasons, attitudes, and expectations; and, second, that much of their time and thought is devoted to unobtrusive efforts to make these factors as positive as can be achieved.

To sum up this penultimate section, then, within the totality of TEFL there exist a large number of variables, identifiable broadly as relating to the *community,* the *teaching profession* itself, and the *learner.* In addition the nature of the profession's perceptions about its own task changes and develops gradually with the passing of time.

In short, the teacher is like a chameleon. To be efficient, i.e. to survive, the chameleon must continually observe his surroundings and adapt to them. And adapting means *action:* it means selecting from among a range of possible colourings and patterns precisely those which are appropriate to the moment. The teacher, to be efficient—perhaps even to survive—needs to adapt in a similar way: to select from among a wide range of possible techniques and courses of action precisely those which are appropriate to the circumstances of the learning/teaching situation.

Teaching is a hard and emotionally bruising occupation, and language teaching more so than most other specialisms, especially if the language one is teaching is not one's mother tongue. Teachers essentially need two distinct kinds of follow-up to be available to them after and beyond their initial training. One kind of follow-up must be the career-long provision of morale-boosters—of events where teachers can meet together, share ideas, renew acquaintance with success, seek professional commiseration with our little deprivations, and generally break free of the frustrations and annoyances of the daily round; also teachers' associations, workshops, conferences, magazines, and journals, etc., and, for teachers for whom English is not the mother tongue, opportunities to restore and improve their command of the language.

The second kind of follow-up is of a different kind and affects only a proportion of teachers, though again it is essential to the onward development of the profession as a whole. This is the availability of courses of *further training,* with the purpose of developing an adequate higher echelon of senior professionals, teacher trainers, advisers, and consultants.

III. Consequences of this analysis

The argument so far presented is basically a simple one. It is that the profession we belong to is now a great and global one, of vast scope and influence and containing enormous complexities and subtleties. No single one of us, as a teacher, encounters all the possibilities of choice: indeed, most of us live our working lives within a single, fairly simple segment of the whole—we are usually aware of only the big toe of the TEFL elephant, or the tip of its tusk, or its tail, or its trunk. But just as the elephant exists as a complete and complex animal, even if we can see only a part of it, so also TEFL exists and is subject to all the many variables we have been discussing.

But we are teachers. We are members of the total profession of human education. And that places before us the responsibility for knowing what we are doing, for being aware not just of our own little segment of the profession, but (at least in broad outline) of the whole field, of the variables that now exist and of their consequences. What are these consequences?

The first and most obvious consequence is that any lingering nostalgia for a single 'best' method is completely misplaced. No single method can conceivably be equally suitable for all values of all the variables—for all learners, of any age, regardless of aims, of attitudes, of level of proficiency, and so forth.[1]

A second consequence is that the individual teacher needs to acquire the widest and deepest understanding of all the variables he or she is likely to encounter in the language learning/teaching situation where he will be working. The teacher needs to select, devise, and operate, for any given situation, that methodology which has the best fit, the closest match, with all the variables.

Behind the teacher is a third and final consequence of the variables facing us. This is a consequence for the TEFL profession. now that TEFL is so vast, so complex, yet so important, it has become essential for the profession to have corporate ways of observing, monitoring, analysing, and influencing its own development. Hence the vital importance not only of academic centres of excellence such as university departments and teacher-training colleges, not just of resource centres like the Center for Applied Linguistics, the Regional English Language Centre in Singapore, the British Council's English Teaching Information Centre in London, and similar centres elsewhere, but also of professional teachers' organizations—of TESOL, IATEFL, AILA, and the rest—and of their programmes of events. It is in such corporate activities that we learn from each other about variables other than the ones we know of and meet in our ordinary life, i.e. where we exchange experiences and where we discover that the wall, the spear, the snake, the tree, the fan, and the rope, are, in fact, part of an elephant. Our profession becomes daily ever more complex, subtle, sophisticated. We as teachers must learn to adapt, chameleon-like, to an ever-greater array of variables, so that we can offer to our students not a single technique which may or may not be effective, but the best possible choice of teaching for the particular variables that operate in our own students' individual circumstances.

---

[1] If I have any reservation of substance about the claims made for the Silent Way, Community Language Learning, and Suggestopedia, it is that they seem to *claim* to be suitable in all circumstances. I find that to be counter-intuitive and against experience.

Chapter 4

'Practical' Versus 'Academic' in Teaching English: The Descriptive and the Linguistic Traditions

Introduction

Throughout the first three chapters we have referred even-handedly, as it were, both to 'practical' matters such as methodology and classroom needs, and to 'academic' matters such as linguistics and other disciplines. It is, indeed, the author's major personal belief that all the historical stages of EFL—its original emergence, the decades of its professionalisation, and its healthy future development—all owe a great deal to both the 'practical' and the 'academic' types of activity. When one attempts to analyse the great complexity of the global profession and practice of language teaching, by pointing out the principal variables and relationships between them, one is constantly struck by the interplay of 'practical' and 'academic': or rather (because the term 'academic' is both emotive and inaccurate) by the interplay of *action* and *rationale*—by the contribution to teaching which can be made by ideas, provided that they embody sufficient understanding and experience of relevant practicalities.

But that formulation, though I believe it to be just, itself embodies an opinion which is by no means universal, about the inter-dependence of the 'practical' and the 'academic', of 'action' and 'rationale'. It is almost as if those who teach foreign languages, and in particular English, are divided between two ideologies at first sight incompatible. In their extreme form, these ideologies are represented by the opposing views (a) that language teaching is overwhelmingly a matter of practical classroom procedures, with little if anything to learn from 'academic theory', and (b) that, on the contrary, language teaching suffers through an almost total lack of theoretical underpinning and that teachers should undergo rigorous training in (principally) theoretical linguistics.

A more realistic standpoint is provided, not just by the emollient but essentially trivial compromise of asserting that the truth lies somewhere between the two extremes, but by the observation that advances, improvements, and developments in language teaching commonly evolve from two distinct sources: firstly, from creative imagination employed in wrestling with problems that present themselves in practical, 'classroom' terms; and, secondly, from creative imagination engaged in thinking about fundamental principles and *ideas* relevant to the learning and teaching of languages.

Some individuals find one of these sources of development more congenial than the other; some, alas, associate themselves with one of them—the 'practical' or the 'academic'—to the exclusion and denigration of the other; an increasing number recognize the relevance of both, and switch between the one and the other during the course of their careers.

This argument over the roles of principle and theory can be seen as another facet of the long-standing argument about the relation between linguistics and language teaching. In that discussion, too, polemics and emotional commitments tend to obscure objective facts and common sense. And the difficulty of persuading protagonists on either side to become more open to the views of the other is made the greater by the gap in attitudes and even in modes of thought between the two extremes. Those whose training for teaching languages has been solely of the the 'practical' type—whether or not preceded by a training in the humane, response-oriented disciplines of literature—typically experience shock when they come up against two unexpected features of linguistics. These are, firstly, that linguistics is opaque: without training and application, the writings of linguistics cannot be adequately understood. Secondly, that linguistics shares the thought-processes and the attempted precision of the sciences rather than the allusive discourse of the humanities.

Equally, the products of a training in linguistics who then encounter for the first time the attitudes and procedures of practical teacher training typically also experience shock when they come up against two of its unexpected features. These are, firstly, that teaching is hardly at all concerned with the results of research: the bases for procedures lie in assertions, in untested assumptions, in currently accepted attitudes, and modes of action. And, secondly, that the extended exercise of pure intellectual thought is only rarely required of the teacher.

It might seem that the extreme points of view are so far apart as to defy mutual understanding. Yet looking at the historical development of language teaching we can see that from time to time there emerges an authority who becomes accepted by people at both extremes, and whose work demonstrates an alternative to mutual hostility. One such person was A. S. Hornby, who died in 1978, soon after his 80th birthday.

Hornby was at once an experienced practical teacher of English as a foreign language, a contributor to research in contrastive linguistics, a major authority on the grammar and syntax of English, a teacher trainer, a lexicographer and dictionary maker, a syllabus designer, and a writer of teaching materials. He produced authoritative writings which satisfied both the demand for rigour, on the one hand, and the requirement of immediate understanding, on the other.

In this chapter, a group of Hornby's most influential works are discussed, in illustration of ways in which the apparent gulf between 'practical' and 'academic' can be bridged.

I

A recurrent theme in language teaching is the need felt by teachers of English for information *about* the language, as a support and a supplement to their personal, practical command of it. The need is felt by all serious teachers of the language, whether or not they speak English as their mother tongue. Yet it is extremely difficult to specify in detail just what kinds of information meet the need. In one sense, what the teacher seeks is a general understanding of how the language works (so that the need is a broad one, not restricted to words, or to pronunciation, or to grammar), but also a source to which he can turn for precise and detailed and comprehensive information about each of the very many sub-systems within language, from 'the pronunciation of word-final *s* in the plural of regular nouns' to 'the different functions of *have'*, to 'relations between *time* and *tense* in English', to 'classes of verbs and possibilities of object and complement', to 'intonation patterns', and many others. In short, the need is to make both *explicit* and *accessible to the teacher* the knowledge of English possessed by native speakers and advanced learners of the language.

It was not the least of A. S. Hornby's achievements that, recognizing the nature of this need as a result of his personal experience in teaching English, he produced over a period of 30 years a group of major works designed quite specifically to meet it. In particular, the *Oxford Advanced Learner's Dictionary* (in its various forms), the *Guide to Patterns and Usage in English,* and *The Teaching of Structural Words and Sentence Patterns* together form a linked set. They comprise a dictionary—or rather, a family of dictionaries for different types of learner—a grammar (because that is what the *Guide to Patterns and Usage* actually is) and an array of classroom presentation techniques for teaching a large proportion of the grammatical devices of English.

What is more, this set of works, embodying as they do a description of the present-day English language not based on any linguistic theory, was produced during the very period 1935-75 when the discipline of linguistics not only achieved maturity and autonomy but in the case of very many languages became the principal source of new works of linguistic description. Hornby's contribution was a prime and particular example of an interesting general distinction, which applies in relation to English, between two different lines of intellectual development: the *descriptivist* tradition, on the one hand, and the *linguistic* tradition, on the other.

These distinct strands of development are not in an *either/or* relationship: it is not a question of one being 'right' and the other being 'wrong'. But it is helpful to the teacher of English to be aware that both strands exist and to accord to each the respect it deserves, in its own terms. It is just as irrelevant for a teacher of English to complain that (for example) transformational-generative grammar provides insufficient help to the classroom teacher, as it is for a linguist to object that Hornby's *Guide to Patterns and Usage* lacks theoretical adequacy. In their own terms and used for their own purposes, each has a valuable place. More than that, perhaps: a greater awareness of both strands enables the teacher to discern that although TG has nothing to say about classroom methodology it provides many insights into language as the product of the human mind; while, on the other hand, the linguist may come to realize that even though some of the most complex features of English (e.g. the passive) cannot yet be satisfactorily 'explained' in terms of theory, nevertheless they have to be taught in the EFL classroom, and that for this purpose Hornby's work contains simple yet illuminating assistance.

During the past century of teaching English as a foreign language, in fact, *three* lines can be distinguished in the development of materials and reference works (though one of these lines petered out and will be ignored once we have identified it). The three lines are: (i) the 'traditional grammar' line, exemplified by the work of Nesfield: this is the line which has not continued its development to the present day; (ii) the 'descriptivist' line, exemplified in the work of, e.g. Sweet—Jespersen—Palmer—Hornby—Quirk (though one must not suggest that these names form a strict genealogical tree); (iii) the 'linguistic' line, exemplified in the work of, for example, Bloomfield—Fries—Hill—Lado, etc., with a 'loop line' through Chomsky—Roberts—Rutherford, and a separate line to accommodate Sinclair and colleagues, which latter development converges more closely with the 'descriptivist' line.[1]

We are here touching upon the chronology of linguistics, the chronology of English-language studies, the chronology of teaching English as a foreign language, and some of the interactions between these three; and we are considering the interactions from the standpoint of English-language teaching. In broad outline one might characterize the interrelationships in the following way: (i) before

---

[1] It is necessary to point out that the names are selected in order to suggest common or contrasting characteristics but they are certainly not intended to provide a comprehensive list of sources.

1940 the primary sources of awareness of English were, (a) among teachers using grammar-translation methods, 'traditional' grammar; and (b) increasingly, among teachers using direct method and other speech-centred methods, the 'descriptivist' line: the 'linguistic' line, in other words, did not begin to affect language teaching in any major way until after 1940; (ii) since 1940 the primary sources have been: (a) among American-influenced teachers, overwhelmingly from the 'linguistic' tradition; and (b) among British-influenced teachers, from the 'descriptivist' line; (iii) but recently the two lines have begun to converge in ways which we shall consider later.

It is worth noting that the 'descriptivist' line in Britain has always included *phonetics,* both in an academic form as *general phonetics* and in the form of 'the phonetics of English presented so as to help the teacher'. Indeed, in Britain the tradition of academic phonetics developed by Professor Daniel Jones established a reservoir of scholars knowledgeable about language many of whom became founders of a separate profession of *linguistics* when this developed in the period between 1935 and 1950. Since phonetics had been closely related to foreign-language teaching, this concern was carried over into the early days of linguistics.

After *c.* 1940, interactions between foreign language teaching and linguistics grew apace, especially in the United States, where the 'linguistic' line of development reached its extreme form in the guise of the audio-lingual method. We are concerned here not with the methodological bases of audio-lingual teaching which were adopted with little modification from Skinnerian conditioning theory, nor yet with the course-books written in this mode, but with information *about* English produced for the help and illumination of the teacher. The Bloomfieldian tradition of the period 1940-65 was quite clear about this: to be an adequate teacher of a foreign language it was inescapably necessary to be trained in structuralist linguistics. Thus the 'language awareness' material—if we may use this label to refer to the kinds of reference works we are referring to—which the teacher on the Bloomfieldian 'linguistic' line was expected to use consisted of mainstream analyses of phonetics, phonemics, and morphemics, e.g. by Trager and Smith, Lado, Fries, and Marckwardt, together with a very small amount on sentence-grammar, particularly in the style of A. A. Hill's *Introduction to Linguistic Structures*.

The philosophy of this school of linguistics was that linguistics provides the best description of English, and that conventional classroom methodology should be superseded by instructional techniques derived from Skinner's psychological theories of learning. For at least two reasons we should resist the temptation, offered by hindsight, to be derisive about these views. The first reason is that great success was achieved—and continues to be—using these methods and materials *in the conditions for which they were designed,* i.e. for highly motivated, highly selected, academically bright young adults, taught intensively by highly qualified native English-speaking teachers, trained in linguistics, in an environment where English is the medium of instruction and of the surrounding community. The shortcomings of audio-lingual teaching and of this linguistics-dominated outlook only became apparent when materials of this same type were taught non-intensively to unmotivated, unselected, mixed-ability school children, by poorly qualified non-English-speaking teachers with no training in linguistics, in countries where English was not the language of instruction, nor of the community. In retrospect we can see that the original success of the audio-lingual method was not, as was claimed, its basis in linguistics and psychology (i.e. Bloomfieldian linguistics and Skinnerian psychology). But neither was the subsequent lack of success due to Bloomfieldian structural linguistics being 'bad' linguistics and Skinnerian psychology being 'poor' psychology. The success had been because the teaching materials well fitted one particular learning-teaching situation; and the failure was because the same materials did not suit a totally different learning-teaching situation.

The second reason for not being scornful about the audio-lingual era is that by the lights of 1950, in the United States, these ideas and materials constituted a real advance on most of what had there preceded them. And in the last analysis the best that any of us can hope for, professionally speaking, is not to attain perfection but to perceive some modest way of improving upon what has gone before.

Keeping our attention for the moment on this American line of development, the rapid decline of Bloomfieldian linguistics and the rise to domination in its place of Chomsky's theoretical ideas caused great problems for teachers of English. Not only was the tradition of linguistics within which they had been trained and which they believed to embody their hopes of success suddenly overturned, but worse: the revolution was a highly polemical one, so that Bloomfieldian linguistics was not just superseded, it was positively reviled. Skinnerian psychology was similarly attacked, along with all its works. And to make matters even more distressing, Chomsky made it clear on a number of occasions that he saw little relevance for language teaching in his own theoretical standpoint, or in psychology as it was then composed.[1]

Nevertheless, the connection with linguistics was so strongly entrenched in American language teaching that Paul Roberts, W. E. Rutherford, and others pursued a line in which a TG view of linguistics replaced a structuralist one, with a 'cognitive-code' outlook on learning and teaching superseding the mechanistic methodology of audiolingual teaching. What of 'language awareness' sources of reference during this period? A new difficulty arose: one of the central tenets of transformational-generative theory is that the task of linguistics is not to describe languages but to explain the human faculty of language. The production of works of reference for teachers is rendered especially difficult by this point of view, and the problem is made worse by the greater abstraction of TG linguistics compared with structuralist linguistics, as well as by the use of a sophisticated notational system, so that teachers now required (but hardly ever received) additional, specialized training in linguistics before they could comprehend and use such descriptive materials as were prepared according to the TG model. In short, the greater theoretical rigour of Chomskyan linguistics, quite apart from its preoccupation with syntax and with an orientation towards cognitive psychology, led to a reduction in the immediate practical relevance of linguistics for language teachers, and consequently to the production of few 'language awareness' materials of the kind we are considering.

[1]For a more detailed discussion of these matters see Chapters 1 and 5 in Strevens, P., *New Orientations in the Teaching of English,* Oxford University Press, 1977.

We have looked in some detail at the 'linguistics' line as it developed in the United States. In Britain, the history was different in a number of ways. To begin with, Bloomfieldian linguistics and Skinnerian psychology was never dominant in Britain, so that any attractions which audio-lingual teaching might have possessed were confined to methodology and to their reputation for success in practice: the 'theological' appeal had little force in Britain. Rather the contrary: linguistics in Britain from 1930 onwards had close ties with the Prague School of linguistics, whose philosophy has always been concerned with language as a social phenomenon.[1] Linguists in Britain generally pride themselves on being aware of schools of thought in linguistics throughout the world, no matter which theoretical position the individual linguist may prefer. In addition, the theoretical viewpoint of J. R. Firth (1957a, 1957b) and his co-workers has been influential, with its inclusion of meaning, of social role, of phonetics and phonology, and of lexis, as well as of grammar. And Firthian linguistics accepts the description of languages as one of the central tasks of linguistics (not the only task, by any means, but certainly one to be pursued among others).

Here we must refer once again to the rise since 1960 of a cross-disciplinary approach to the solution of language-based problems. This approach, usually known as *applied linguistics,* deliberately selects, from among *all* the relevant disciplines—linguistics, psychology, educational theory, social theory, etc.—those elements which are of greatest illumination to language problems, including language teaching. It is also the case that many British linguists, in addition to virtually all applied linguists, have chosen to involve themselves in practical problems of syllabus design, production of materials, etc., quite apart from their contributions on the theoretical plane. It is this 'activist' outlook that accounts for the contributions of M.A.K. Halliday and J. McH. Sinclair, among others, to the 'linguistic' line of development referred to earlier. For example, Sinclair's *A Course in Spoken English: Grammar* (Oxford University Press, 1972) is at one and the same time a teaching text for both

[1]Note the implications in the title of Fried, V. (ed.), *The Prague School of Linguistics and Language Teaching,* Oxford University Press, 1972.

foreign and native English-speaking students, a descriptive grammar of present-day spoken English, and an exemplification of systemic linguistic theory; M. A. K. Halliday's volume in the same series, *A Course in Spoken English: Intonation,* has a similar function, but concentrates on intonation.[1]

There is, however, one interesting feature about this recent British extension of the 'linguistic' line of development, namely that no prior training in linguistics is needed on the part of the teacher or the student in order to understand and use these materials. Earlier in this chapter it was suggested that the principal need is for information to be *explicit,* and also to be *accessible.* Many of the materials produced on the 'linguistics' line were explicit: they incorporated detailed information about how English works. But in most cases the information was not accessible without special training in linguistics, with the notable exception of the Halliday-Sinclair branch of the 'linguistic' line. In that sense, they converge with the 'descriptivist' line, to which we now turn.

The 'descriptivist' tradition, exemplified in the work of Sweet, Jespersen, Palmer, Hornby, Zandvoort, Quirk, and others, has always been both explicit and accessible. It began long before linguistics emerged as an autonomous discipline and it continues today. However, it is an error to assume (as some people unfortunately do) that this tradition is unaware of, or unaffected by, developments in linguistics over the past 50 years. The descriptivist tradition is independent of linguistics, but it is assuredly neither against linguistics nor ignorant of it. The ideal relationship between the two is best illustrated by the following quotation from the greatest modern example of the tradition, *A Grammar of Contemporary English,* by R. Quirk, S. Greenbaum, G. Leech, and J. Svartvik (Longman, 1972):

> 'It will be obvious that our grammatical framework has drawn heavily both on the long-established tradition and on the insights of several contemporary schools of linguistics. But while we have taken account of modern linguistic theory to the extent that we think

[1]The third book in this series, *A Course in Spoken English: Texts, Drills, and Exercises,* is written by R. Mackin.

justifiable in a grammar of this kind, we have not felt that this was the occasion for detailed discussion of theoretical issues. Nor do we need to justify the fact that we subscribe to no specific one of the current or recently formulated linguistic theories. Each of those propounded from the time of de Saussure and Jespersen onwards has its undoubted merits, and several (notably the transformational-generative approaches) have contributed very great stimulus to us as to other grammarians. None, however, seems yet adequate to account for all linguistic phenomena, and recent trends suggest that our own compromise position is a fair reflection of the way in which the major theories are responding to influence from others.'[1]

II

The lessons to be drawn from the foregoing outline of the two main lines would seem to be that each has validity in its own terms, that neither can claim inherent superiority over the other, and that while the teacher of English will find illumination in both, within the 'linguistic' tradition he may find difficulty in gaining access to the insights that are potentially available there.

What of Hornby's particular contribution to the 'descriptivist' tradition? To speak only briefly of the merits of the *Oxford Advanced Learner's Dictionary,* quite apart from the lexical, lexicogrammatical, and phonetic information incorporated within the body of the dictionary there exists also an invaluable Introduction of 27 pages, containing in the third edition useful information about the principles used in preparing the dictionary entries, word-division, specialist usage, pronunciation, and stress, and (above all) a summary of verb patterns; and also ten appendices, totalling 32 pages, listing such handy data as abbreviations, numerical expressions, weights and measures, names of Shakespeare's works, ranks in the armed forces, and books of the Bible. The dictionary is much more than simply a dictionary.

---

[1]Not all linguists accept this point of view, and some maintain that the work of Quirk and his colleagues would have been even more valuable if it had been based upon a single theoretical position. Arguments of this 'if only' type are unlikely ever to be resolved. In the meantime the Quirk *et al. Grammar* will long reign as the most comprehensive descriptive grammar of the present-day English language.

The *Guide to Patterns and Usage,* too, is much more than it seems, being in fact a partial grammar of English. It is based on an analysis of surface structure and is basically an aide-memoire for teachers and advanced students. In its own terms, it is fairly comprehensive. Features such as the *passive, negation, emphasis,* and *interrogation* receive little treatment, but, on the other hand, the final section of the book is entitled 'Various Concepts and Ways in which they are Expressed'; in it there is a unique series of explanations and illustrations of how the following are treated in English:

> Commands, instructions, requests, invitations.
>   suggestions, prohibitions
> Permission
> Probability and likelihood
> Possibility
> Ability and achievement (and their opposites)
> Intention
> Plans and arrangements
> Obligations and necessity
> Determination and resolve; willingness
> Promises, threats, refusals
> Wishes, hopes, preferences
> Purpose and result
> Cause, reason, result
> Comparisons and contrasts
> Concession
> Conditions and suppositions

In Hornby's own view, the central contribution contained within the *Guide* was probably his verb patterns (25 in the first edition, expanded to 27 in the second). These patterns are concerned with the combinations of *Subject—Verb—Direct Object—Indirect Object* and other additions such as noun/pronoun (phrase), and the like. Five of the patterns relate to verbs used intransitively; the remaining 22 relate to verbs used transitively. Other analyses are possible, but Hornby's represents a remarkable boiling-down of the great complexity of verbal patternings in English. For readers not familiar with the *Guide,* the facsimile page (Fig. 1) will illustrate the principle and at the same time show what an enormous quantity of additional detail is given by way of the tables and examples.

TABLE No. 64

Summary of Material in §§ 203-204

These	books	are	all both	mine.
		all both	belong to me.	
	bags			
They		are	both all	working hard. playing football.
		have		gone to London. read this book
	both all		speak English well like oranges.	

TABLE No. 65

Summary of Material in § 205

What else	is there in the box? did you do? does he want?		
There is	something nothing	else	here in my bag
Is there	anything		

Fig. 1.

Finally, *The Teaching of Structural Words and Sentence Patterns*. This, the third in Hornby's trilogy, almost defies a summary description. In 4 paperback volumes (now printed in 3 books) of under 500 pages in total, Hornby gives the teacher detailed instructions for practical ways of presenting in class a great many of the basic points about English. Figure 2 is a page from the summary of contents of Stage III.

The Teaching of Structural Words and Sentence Patterns (*TOSWASP* as it is widely called) is a quite unparalleled source of shrewd and effective guidance for the teacher about ways of successfully teaching several hundred features of the English language. Its influence over the past two decades has been immense, as a model for teachers and teacher trainers throughout the world, and also as the origin (often, alas, unacknowledged) of material and techniques incorporated in many subsequent textbooks.

Hornby's work, then, epitomizes this 'descriptivist' line of development. Being lucidly expressed, packed with self-evidently wise practical advice, and above all accessible to even the weakest teacher with little or no professional training, ASH's contributions have been to make plain the English language to the teacher, so that the teacher in turn can make it plain to the learner.

Yet the very clarity and accessibility of ASH's work has sometimes produced a curious and unwanted by-product. Alongside the undoubted pedagogical and methodological qualities of excellence that exist in British ELT (and indeed in the teaching of foreign languages also) there has often appeared an anti-intellectual streak. If it was true that in American TEFL in the 1950s the slogan 'Make them structural linguists and the teaching will look after itself' led to concentration on the linguistics to the detriment of pedagogy, in British ELT there was, and persists, a converse tendency to say 'Give them practical techniques and the ideas will look after themselves'. And when a very proper concern with *pedagogical professionalism* (as contrasted with the *disciplinary professionalism* more characteristic of American TEFL—see Strevens, 1978a) is taken to extremes, it can lead to a disdain for theoretical notions of any kind and hence to the establish-

Verb Pattern 4

1.61   Transitive verbs are used with a *to*-infinitive: this is
VP7. Intransitive verbs are also used with a *to*-
infinitive, as in VP4. The pattern is subdivided.

[VP4A] 1.62   The infinitive is one of purpose, outcome, or
result.

Table 29

	subject + *vi*	*to*-infinitive (phrase)
1	*We stopped*	*to have a rest.*
2	*We went*	*to hear the concert.*
3	*He got up*	*to answer the phone.*
4	*She stood up*	*to see better.*
5	*Someone has called*	*to see you.*
6	*They ran*	*to help the injured man.*
7	*I come*	*to bury Caesar, not to priase him.*
8	*He came*	*to see that he was mistaken.*
9	*How do you come*	*to know that?*
10	*Now that I come*	*to think of it . . .*
11	*How can I get*	*to know her?*
12	*The swimmer failed*	*to reach the shore.*
13	*Will he live*	*to be ninety?*
14	*I hope I live*	*to see men on Mars.*
15	*The people grew*	*to believe that she was a witch.*
16	*We stand*	*to lose a large sum of money.*
17	*It was so dark we couldn't see*	*to read.*

Note

In sentences 1 to 7, *to = in order to,* indicating purpose.
8 may be paraphased: *He eventually saw that he was mistaken,*
or *The time came when he saw that he was mistaken.*
11 means *How can I make her acquaintance?*
16 means *We are in a position where we may lose a large sum
of money.*

Fig. 2.

ment of teacher-training programmes almost devoid of any intellectual content. Why bother with courses on grammar, let alone linguistics (the argument runs) when the nature of English is made plain to all in Hornby's work, together with clear instructions on how to teach the language?

The error in such an attitude is twofold. In the first place, professionalism in language teaching requires that the teacher understands *why?* as well as knowing *what?* and *how?*—it is an educational error to train language teachers as if they were garage mechanics rather than engineers (if a partial analogy may be permitted). But in the second place, such an attitude overlooks the very considerable intellectual achievement that underlies the descriptivist line, just as it does the linguistic line. To pursue the analogy, Hornby's work is like good engineering, clearly expressed so as to be accessible not only to other engineers but also to mechanics—but it is like *good* engineering because it also stems from a deep understanding of the laws of physics, i.e. of the principles and the laws of the universe of discourse within which the language teacher works.

The 'linguistic' and the 'descriptivist' lines have this in common, whatever differences there may be between their ultimate aims: they both have their origins in scholarship and in the application of intellect. Hornby's contribution in making plain the English language for the teacher of English is indeed immediately accessible to the classroom practitioner, but its greater quality has been to provide, as do others in this tradition, a fuller understanding, based on scholarly principles, of the English language of today.

The same bridge-building concept should apply throughout language teaching. Instead of contrasting *either* 'practical' *or* 'academic', language teachers can come to realize that both have their place, that the place of each is different, and that what really matters is the application of intelligence at *every* point along the scale between *action* and *rationale*.

Part II

PERSPECTIVES ON ENGLISH
AS AN INTERNATIONAL LANGUAGE

Chapter 5

The Expansion of English and the Emergence of Localized Forms of English

I. Introduction: the nature of the problem

It is commonly accepted that the English language is vastly more used nowadays than it was in the past, and that the expansion of its use continues apace. Yet, paradoxically, as this one single language expands the diversity of forms within the total envelope of 'English' also increases: 'more use of English' is accompanied by 'more different kinds of English'. The increase in diversity of forms brings in its wake a number of new anxieties and problems for the users of English, especially for non-native speakers of the language, and, above all, for those concerned with language education.

These anxieties are related to doubts about criteria for the acceptability of different forms of English, about the maintenance of international mutual intelligibility in English, about value judgements on various 'non-native' forms, about technical problems of description and typology, and about problems of the educational suitability of some forms of English.

II. The expansion of English and some consequential problems

1. The expansion of English.

Three kinds of expansion need to be recognized,
i.e. expansion in:

(a) Number of users of English.

(b) Range of uses of English.

(c) Number of local forms of English.

Each of these contributes to the circumstances under discussion, but in differing ways.

(a) *Expansion in number of users of English.* It is estimated (Bowen, 1975) that the number of those who use English now exceeds 600 million, of whom about 300 million are native speakers while another 300 million are users who have 'picked up' the language or have learned it through formal instruction to a level where they can use it for some purpose or other, however limited and instrumental. These figures make it likely that English has the biggest number of non-native users of any of the world's languages.

(b) *Expansion in range of uses of English.* Every language displays a range of uses employed by its native speakers; in the majority of cases when a language is taught to (or acquired by) foreigners, only a restricted subset of these uses are transferred, and no new ones are likely to appear. As *foreign* languages, most languages have a very restricted range of uses. English, by contrast, serves in many countries in addition to or instead of local languages as a vehicle for science, for the mass media (press, radio, television), and some kinds of international entertainment, and to some extent for literature. Of course, a very large number of languages other than English serve as vehicles for these activities, too, but on the whole *only in their own country* and for native speakers, whereas English serves these purposes for non-native speakers in most of the countries where it is used. In addition, the use of English for purely local purposes (e.g. certain uses of English in India) creates new circumstances unknown in the 'mother-tongue' situation.

(c) *Expansion in the number of localized forms of English.* By localized forms of English (LFE) is meant the proliferation of identifiable forms of English, embraced in preference to all others, by a major section of a particular English-using community. Thus, for example, the existence of Singapore English, Malta English, Zambian English, Hong Kong English, etc., are all examples of this trend. It should be noted that whereas 25 years ago the existence of these forms of English would have been conceded defensively, if not defiantly, by those who use them, nowadays they are accepted as being in a certain sense the manifestation of local cultural identity, even though English is not the mother tongue of any but an atypical handful of the inhabitants.

2. *New causes for concern.*

In using the expression 'causes for concern' it is essential to make the point that these are concerns actually felt and expressed by users of English, both native speakers and non-native speakers. It is not that there exists some generalized state of emergency that threatens the language: rather that quite specific reasons for anxiety, doubt, or uncertainty nowadays face people who previously had no dubieties about English. Leaving aside the professional aspects of such problems, as expressed by educational specialists and Anglicists (discussed below), two types of concern may be distinguished, relating respectively to (a) *international intelligibility,* and (b) *value-judgements about acceptability.*

(a) *Concern over international intelligibility.* A form which this concern often takes is the question: Will other speakers of English understand us? One of the strongest virtues of English as an international language is that those who use it for purposes of international communication can comprehend each other in both its written and its spoken forms. But the extent of variation that can exist without impairing mutual intelligibility is by no means obvious; many people jump to the extreme and unwarranted conclusion that local variation is inherently undesirable for this reason, regardless of whether it may have other advantages.

(b) *Concern over value-judgements of acceptability.* The myth of a single 'golden' or 'pure' form of English dies hard. Echoes of the past, when only native-speaker varieties—the English of those for whom it is the mother tongue—were acceptable among educated speakers, are still to be heard; the irrational view that since Shakespeare (or Wordsworth, Dickens, etc) was the greatest writer in the English language, and since he came from England, therefore only the English of England is acceptable, is still expressed in some places. Even among communities where it is recognized that a local form of English (especially a locally identifiable accent) is a desirable means of expressing social and cultural identity, there remains a widespread apprehension that variation from mother-tongue forms may lead to judgements that these variations embody a 'second-class' English, at least in the eyes of some English-users.

3. Professional problems

The concerns touched on above are those often articulated by the non-specialist public. But those engaged in academic studies of English, too—including those in the teaching of English as a foreign language, in teacher training and other apposite branches of education, in applied linguistics and sociolinguistics—acknowledge new problems as a result of the expansion of English and the proliferation of new forms of the language. These problems can be summarized as being related to *description, typology,* and *educational suitability.*

(a) *Problems of description.* With few exceptions, only native-speaker forms of English have been described in a tolerably comprehensive way, and although much effort within sociolinguistics is currently being devoted to the description and explanation of diversity, it seems that the proliferation of forms of English is taking place faster than the description of them. It is, of course, extremely difficult to produce a comprehensive description of *any* form of language: the sheer quantity, intensity, and stamina of intellectual effort involved can be divined from a study of, for example, Quirk *et al., Grammar of Contemporary English.* To produce even a tiny proportion of that massive achievement for each of a score of other forms of English would be a hefty undertaking. Nevertheless, once a form of English is identified as having an existence it cries out to be described, at least in its essential or differential features.

(b) *Problems of typology.* Beyond the questions of describing each individual form there arises the question of relationships between different 'Englishes': similarities, differences, reasons for common or divergent features, etc. At the present time some local forms of English are being considered in terms of typology, particularly from the valuable standpoint of studies of *creolization* and *pidginization*. But much remains to be explained outside the domain of any single discipline.

(c) *Problems of educational suitability.* The emergence of a newly identified form of English brings with it problems as to its suitability for use as a model. If 'educated Nigerian English' exists as a recognizable, identifiable entity, should that form become the model and target used in the teaching of English in the schools of Nigeria? (See Chapter 7.) If so, what steps are needed in the production of teaching materials, in teacher training, in testing and examining? If a local form is *not* used, what attitudes towards it should teachers adopt, and how could and should they justify the use of a model derived from elsewhere? These and many other problems of great difficulty and yet of prime importance are raised by the proliferation of forms of English.

4. *An approach to these concerns and problems.*

It is not realistic to suppose that all these difficulties can be solved by a single, simple solution. A first step towards at least the understanding of the underlying nature of the difficulties, however, is the analysis of the principal parameters of variety. These are summarized in Table 1 and discussed in detail in section III below.

III. Parameters defining and differentiating local forms of English

The expression 'local form of English' is intended as a technical term to refer to an identifiable version of English associated with a given community of English users. A term additional to the well-established terms 'dialect' and 'accent' is required in order to designate the particular profile or mixture of five distinct variables.

Local forms of English vary in two ways: firstly, according to a profile of variables that describes their formal nature in linguistic terms; secondly, according to their use and function, broadly interpreted. In the analysis that follows these two kinds of parameter are labelled 'defining' and 'differentiating' respectively. The former set determines a particular local form of English, the later set differentiates one LFE from another.

TABLE 1. Parameters of variety

Group A. *DEFINING PARAMETERS*
       (i.e. parameters defining particular local forms of English)

1. Dialect and accent
2. Range of varieties
3. Discoursal rules   Local forms
4. Existence of 'standard' and   of English
    non-standard forms   derive from
5. Primary-language and   profiles
    secondary-language forms   of A1-6
    (L1/L2)
6. Foreign language/second
    language forms: (FL/SL)

Group B: *DIFFERENTIATING PARAMETERS*
       (i.e. parameters that differentiate between different local forms of english)

1. Status and uses in the community

2. Whether the vehicle for:
    (a) public education
    (b) science and technology
    (c) international news, entertainment, publicity
    (d) literature

3. Attitudes of the local intellectual and educational leaders

4. Socio-cultural affinities and aversions:
    (a) geographical
    (b) historical
    (c) socio-political
    (d) cultural

Discussion

Group A: Defining parameters

1. Dialect and accent

The combination of these two features carries indexical information about geographical provenance and social/educational background. Differences of *accent* are phonological in nature; differences of *dialect* are grammatical and/or lexical. In the great majority of cases, dialects and accents are paired, so that local dialect X is always spoken in accent X, dialect Y in accent Y, and vice versa; never dialect X with accent Y, and so forth. However, it is a characteristic of English (and I believe it occurs also in other international languages of widespread currency) that one dialect at least ('Standard English': see below) is not localized and is observed to be spoken with virtually any accent. Within most English-using communities one is likely to find individuals using each of the following:

(i)   Local dialect with local accent.
(ii) Standard English with non-localizable accent (e.g. 'RP' in Britain, 'General American' in the United States.)
(iii) Standard English with local accent.

And probably the majority of people will have competence in more than one of these combinations. The central point is that a local form of English is formally defined by the particular mixtures of dialect and accent which it displays.

In normal social intercourse, it is the evidence of dialect and accent that is used by all English users as a first and primary defining criterion: 'I know where you come from and I make some conclusions about your social and educational background on the basis of your dialect and accent.'

2. *Lectal and varietal range*
Other dimensions of variety exist, notably *lectal range* and *varietal range.*

(i) *Lectal range.* Each LFE has its own characteristic range between *acrolect, mesolect,* and *basilect,* and its own social interpretations of when each is appropriate and by people of what role in society.

(ii) *Varietal range.* Allied to lectal range yet distinct from it is the range of varieties available in a given LFE. The range includes, in particular.

(a)   *registers* (roughly, variety according to topic and subject matter, which may be manifested in *phonology,* in *grammar,* in *lexis,* and in *rhetoric,* and is usually visible in a mixture of all four);

    (b) a *formality-familiarity* dimension (in which the degree of formality of the situation and the degree of personal and social familiarity between the participants jointly affect the choice of language actually employed);

    (c) The *appropriacy of slang, colloquialism, swearing, abuse, endearments,* etc., and the rules about when these are acceptable for use by different groups of people.

These three ranges are of considerable extent and subtlety, and they form part of learned social behaviour within particular communities. Consequently they permit large and easily identified distinctions between one LFE and another.

3. *Discoursal rules*

Differences exist between LFEs as to the procedures for achieving a particular illocutionary force, rules for joining and opting out of conversation, techniques for persuasion, mechanisms for regulating social discourse. These differences reflect to a varying degree the equivalent usages in the society concerned, as when an Indian interacts in English to a person he conceives as a Guru, or a Japanese works out how he uses English when he is joined, during a conversation with foreigners, by other Japanese of a social status clearly different from his own.

The pragmatics of discourse seem to be prone to display features transferred from local culture in the same way as pronunciation does. This is perhaps not surprising: the pragmatics of discourse constitute a major part of our rules for regulating both interpersonal relations in general and at the same time the subtle ways in which we express our own requirements and understand what other human beings are doing. Such rules are learned within our particular culture from a very early age—certainly before mastery of language—and over a long period, perhaps one's entire lifetime. Yet they are made explicit only very rarely. Consequently we tend, as learners of a foreign language, to be only dimly aware, if at all, that the rules of discourse for using a foreign language in its cultural setting will be different from those of our native language. As teachers of a foreign language, we are only recently beginning to describe, and hardly at all as yet to incorporate into teaching materials, the rules for constructing discourse, for taking and ceding a turn, for producing with our language a desired effect through choice and manipulation of illocutionary force, and so forth. The point at issue is that local forms of English vary in the detail of their discoursal rules; the appropriate set of detailed rules is an essential defining feature.

4. *Existence of 'standard' and non-standard forms*

Languages used by very large populations with great geographical dispersion frequently exhibit a tendency to develop one dialect (possibly two over a whole continent) which breaks free from the normal localized nature of dialects and their paired accents, and which assumes a role as a 'standard' dialect. This role is social in its origin; the language of a dominant clan, or social class, or educational/intellectual community, becomes accepted as a kind of reference point or norm. In the case of English—and it must be stressed that we are referring to the language in a global sense, not simply to British English—one dialect, and only one, uniquely possesses the following characteristics: (i) it is spoken with pretty well any accent and has no obligatory 'paired' accent of its own; (ii) it is encountered with only trivial variation throughout the English-using world (we are referring here to grammar and lexis, it should be recalled, and not to pronunciation); (iii) it is almost universally accepted by native speakers of English as a suitable model of English for teaching their own young and for teaching foreign learners. This dialect is the one known to linguists and the English-language teaching profession as 'Standard English'.

In LFEs having a wide lectal range, the acrolect typically consists of Standard English with a local accent together with an admixture of some local expressions. The importance of Standard English as an item in this catalogue of features is simply that it plays a greater or a lesser part in one LFE compared with another: the extent of use and acceptance of Standard English is part of the defining characteristics of an LFE.

In this definition, 'Standard English' is the name for what which is constant and similar in the written usage—although obviously it exists in speech also and can be made plain by transliterating spoken discourse into written form—of educated English users in every country: it is the label for those features that enable, for example, British and Americans to understand each other and to exhibit in their grammar and lexis only trivial differences (Strevens, 1972).

Within American English there is a special case to be observed: 'Black English'. In the language of the black community in the United States, Black English occupies a place rather similar to that of Standard English within English as a whole, on the foregoing analysis, since Black English is a non-local dialect that is spoken with local accents. In Black English, the dialect is distributed ethnically but the accents in which it is spoken are distributed geographically. The local accents used by black speakers are similar in many ways to, yet crucially different from, the local accents of whites. Thus, when they have the necessary experience to do so, people immediately recognize from an accent, even when the dialect is Standard English, not only where the speaker comes from but also whether he or she is white or black. (However, the matter is complicated by other general ethnic differentiations such as characteristic voice quality.)

A high proportion of users of Standard English, black or white, are bi-dialectal or multi-dialectal—they switch from one dialect to another and from one accent to another, without conscious decision, according to the social situation within which they find themselves.

Note that 'standard' here does *not* imply 'imposed', nor yet 'of the majority'. One interesting aspect of Standard English is that in every English-using community those who habitually use *only* Standard English are in a minority: that is to say, over the global population of English-users monodialectal Standard English-users are in a very small minority.

The phenomenon of Standard English exists and maintains itself without any conscious or co-ordinated programme of standardization—unlike the position for French, which has its Académie Française as the presumed guardian of the purity of the language. I surmise that Standard English, like 'standard' forms in other languages, is one product of fundamental psycho-social mechanisms, by means of which both the cohesion and the hierarchies of society are roughly paralleled within language.

However that may be, local forms of English have to be considered in relation to Standard English as well as to their own nature. In many places the outcome is very like that which exists, in for example, Britain or North America: an 'internationally high-valued form' occurs, consisting of Standard English spoken with an identifiable local accent, with a small admixture of local expressions and vocabulary; in addition, the majority of the English-using population uses a dialect of more or less local type with local accents. It is presumably the former, an 'internationally high-valued form', that was referred to by Tongue (1974): 'Singapore's Representative to the United Nations, T. T. B. Koh, recently pointed out: ". . . when one is abroad, in a bus or train or aeroplane and when one overhears someone speaking, one can immediately say this is someone from Malaysia or Singapore. And I should hope that when I'm speaking abroad my countrymen will have no problem recognizing that I am a Singaporean." '

5. Primary/secondary forms

This variable relates to the status of the language for the individual user. The *primary language* (L1) of an individual is the one (or more than one) first acquired; all others ever acquired or learned by that individual are *secondary languages*. It is a remarkable feature of English that probably more communication takes place between L2 users of it than between L1 users. As Kachru (1976b) says, referring to 'Third World countries such as the Indian sub-continent, the West Indies or Africa': 'In these countries English is used to teach and maintain the indigenous patterns of life and culture, to provide a link in culturally and linguistically pluralistic societies, and to maintain a continuity and uniformity in educational, administrative and legal systems.' That being so, it seems obvious that different attitudes towards the language will occur among L2 users compared with L1 users, including attitudes towards English in education

6. Foreign-language/second-language forms

Whereas the L1/L2 distinction relates to the individual user of English, the foreign-language/second-language (FL/SL) distinction applies to communities of English users. The distinction is social and educational with historical origins. Where it is taught as a *foreign* language, English has no special status in the community; it is taught as a *second* language in countries where it does have special status. This special status may take any of several forms (e.g. accepted as an official language in administration or the courts of law; the medium of instruction for some parts of the public education system; given major time allocations in local broadcasting systems; etc.).

This distinction is reflected in the acronyms used in British English in relation to the teaching of English outside Britain. EFL means 'English as a foreign language', ESL means 'English as a second language' abroad—though in recent years by extension of this meaning ESL is now the term used to refer to the teaching of English to immigrants in both Britain and North America.

The FL/SL distinction has very real practical importance for the teaching of English (Strevens, 1977a). In EFL countries it is usual for the educational model to be a native-speaker L1 form (e.g. British, American, Australian, etc) and for only a small proportion of learners to reach a high standard; in SL countries there is a tendency for a much higher proportion of learners to reach a level of 'local practical communication' and for a local form of English to be increasingly acceptable as the educational model and target (chapter 7). Furthermore, the importance accorded to evidence of the learner's L1 showing through into his learning of English ('interference errors') is often much greater in EFL—and more heavily penalized—than in ESL conditions.

To sum up, the nature of any local form of English is defined by the profile of particular values of the five foregoing variables. But in addition to their description, forms of English are differentiated from each other by a further set of variables relating to uses, attitudes, and affinities within the English-using community.

Group B: Differentiating parameters

1. *Status and uses in the community*
Here we are thinking of the general public rather than just of the intellectual and educational community. It is obvious that English

possesses different status and uses in, for example, Quebec and Nairobi, although in both cases English is a *second* language. In Quebec the average standard of performance in English may be higher than in Nairobi, and the range of uses for which English is employed may be more extensive; the public status of the language is very different in the two cases. In Nairobi, English is an acceptable instrument of communication within a multi-cultural community, as well as outwards to other countries in Africa and the rest of the world. In Quebec, English is the focus of bitter emotions and political passions, and for many people it has become the symbol of the domination within Canada of French speakers by English speakers. Every English-using community has its own particular range of uses and status within that community.

2. *Whether English is the vehicle for certain uses*

Among L2 English-using communities, English may or may not be used to a significant extent as a vehicle for certain uses: *education, public administration, science and technology, the mass media, international entertainment and publicity,* and *literature.* The first of these is somewhat different from the others: nevertheless, the four seem to make up a coherent set.

(a) *As a vehicle for public education.* This relates not solely to whether English is the medium of instruction in university, secondary, or primary public education, but also to whether major public lectures, seminars, conferences, broadcasts, etc., are customarily offered in English in the certainty that a sufficient audience of local people can and will attend or understand them.

(b) *As a vehicle for public administration.* There are a number of independent countries where English is not an indigenous language which nevertheless use English as either the sole language or one of several languages in the administration of government, the law, the civil service, the police, etc. (The same is true, elsewhere, of French.)

(c) *As a vehicle for science and technology.* It is a feature of Western science and technology that although many of the world's languages serve adequately and even elegantly as a vehicle for expressing and discussing matters of science, not all of them do so. English is one of those which does, perhaps to a greater extent than any other. A consequence of this state of affairs is that in many countries the scientific community switches into English when serving scientific purposes. In other countries, French, German, Spanish, Portuguese, Russian, etc., may serve the same purpose. In the context of an analysis of forms of English, then, we note that one differentiating feature is whether or not English forms the vehicle for science and technology.

(d) *As a vehicle for the mass media, international entertainment, and publicity.* Somewhat analogous to the case of science is what occurs with the press, radio, television, and the cinema. Although, of course, there exists in virtually every community a well-developed media industry operating in the country's own language or languages, at the same time an international, English-language extension of that multi-headed industry also exists. As the level of public command of English rises, so English is used more and more for these purposes. Indeed, the two feed each other: more English-language magazines, etc., lead to a wider spread of at least minimal competence in English, and vice versa. The same applies to certain international entertainment and to some branches of advertising, publicity, and marketing.

(e) *As a vehicle for literature.* What is referred to here is not simply the use of English by academic specialists in English literature, but its use either for creative literature or for critical discussion among L2 English users. In Nigeria, for example, and also in India, there has grown up an important literary profession working entirely in English yet created by and for a readership who are not English L1 speakers. Some English-using communities have developed in this way, others have not.

3. *Attitudes of the local intellectual and educational community*

It is not unknown for these to be in conflict with, or at any rate different from, the attitudes of the general public. For instance, there is a considerable use of English in France, including great quantities of linguistic borrowing into the French language, yet the intellectual establishment firmly reject the principle of using English or even borrowing from it, partly on the grounds that French, too, is an international language, a vehicle for science and literature, with an expansionist political history and therefore with L1/L2 and FL/SL variants in existence overseas, and so forth. In short, the attitudes of the intellectual and educational community affect to a considerable extent the nature of a local form of English.

4. *Socio-cultural affinities and aversions*

L2-using communities belong to a great range of cultural traditions, all of them different in crucial ways from the traditions, history, institutions, attitudes, aspirations, of any and all of the English L1 communities. In some ways, then, we must expect to observe the consequences of these differences made manifest through certain affinities and aversions. For example, West Indian English (the label is a simplification; there are many West Indian Englishes), although located on the American side of the Atlantic and although containing some linguistic similarities with (American) Black English, seems to exhibit rather more affinity with British Isles English. The influence of Black English is greater upon (white) American forms of English through entertainment and the media, from whence the influence is felt in British English, too, at least in the ephemeral usage of teenagers, young adults, and middle-aged disc jockeys.

The sources of these affinities and aversions are of four main kinds:
(a) Geographical.
(b) Historical.
(c) Socio-political.
(d) Cultural.

(a) *Geographical.* This is an obvious source of affinity, but not an overriding one, since, for example, political aversion can be stronger than geographical affinity.

(b) *Historical.* Ultimately most of the present LFEs of L2 communities have historical roots. But the course of history is convoluted, and present affinities may wrestle with past aversions, or vice versa, as, for example, in Malaysia (over the future role of English) or Morocco (over the future role of French).

(c) *Sociopolitical.* The youngest Peace Corps volunteer quickly discovers that in L2 English-using communities both the status of English and the choice of a particular branch of English (British or American) is much affected by social and political philosophies and preferences, which in turn may be very different in neighbouring countries.

(d) *Cultural (including religious).* The demand for English for 'instrumental' purposes may compete with or be supported by cultural and religious affinities and aversions. This is particularly true in areas of the world where the ideological temperature is high or where major religious ideas are on the march, e.g. Islam, or communism.

This concludes our survey of the two groups of principal parameters relating to the definition of local forms of English and to the differentiation between them.

IV. Some consequences for language education and teacher training

1. *General*

The complex set of phenomena reported and analysed in this chapter represent the outward signs of massive sociolinguistic change and development. Their consequences for language education and teacher training are correspondingly great. In the most general terms, these changes require an increase in public and professional enlightenment about language, about variety, about English in particular, and especially about the existence and interaction of the parameters outlined above. This enlightenment is needed in order to combat prejudice and ignorance, since matters of language are sorely liable to accrete myths, legends, and old wives' tales, which in turn can lead to social action being taken on totally erroneous grounds.

2. *Professional enlightenment*

That there should be a need for a major campaign of enlightenment for *professionals,* as well as for the public, reflects the continuing inadequacies in the preparation of teachers, teacher trainers, educational administrators, and decision-making officials. In particular, more understanding is needed, among the categories of occupation noted above, of *language*. Not, it should be noted, of *literature* nor of *linguistics*—or rather, only peripherally of linguistics: more centrally, an understanding of the nature of language in terms of the individual, or society, of literacy and education, of literature, of philosophy, of science, of pedagogy, or national development and language planning.

These are difficult prescriptions, but they are not impossible and are already being approached in some countries. They entail, firstly, a basic change in the nature of the first degree normally required of an intending teacher of English, so that this will no longer be solely concerned with literature but should bring out in the student a sensitive awareness of the nature of language in general and of English in particular, including some familiarity with its phonetic/phonological, grammatical/syntactic, lexical, and semantic mechanisms; secondly, a basic change in the nature of the specialist initial training given to a teacher so as to include a understanding of the ways in which teaching can and cannot be helpful, and the ways in which the community's sociolinguistic ideas and conditions affect the learning and teaching of languages; and, thirdly, a great increase in the availability of further, specialist training for experienced teachers, to give them a deeper understanding of the related disciplines and to help them to be ready for service as advisers, syllabus designers, materials writers, teacher trainers, and so forth. In short, this is a plea for more 'language' in the BA degree, more 'language education' in the teacher training course, and more 'applied linguistics' in the higher degree courses.

As for *popular* enlightenment, this is equally important. Language teaching policy derives its ultimate sanction and justification from the 'public will' (see Strevens, 1978a); consequently the more rapidly change occurs the more essential it is that the public will should be informed and enlightened in matters of language. One of the basic duties of the professionals is to keep the public informed: hence the interlaced importance of these two aspects of enlightenment.

V. Conclusion

The general thesis of this chapter, then, is that English has increased vastly in the quantity and range of its use, that this increase has been accompanied by a proliferation of forms of English, that these events have produced doubts and anxieties among professionals and the general public alike, that the manifold forms of English can best be grasped by an analysis of the multiple variables that define and differentiate them, and that there are great tasks ahead of us in the further and continuing enlightenment of our fellow professionals and of the general public of which we are part.

Chapter 6

International and Intranational Forms of English

I. Introduction

A central problem of linguistic study is how to reconcile a convenient fiction (the notion of 'a language'—'English', 'Chinese', 'Navajo', 'Kashmiri', etc.) with a great mass of inconvenient facts (the mass of diversity exhibited in the actual performance of individuals and communities when they use a given language).

In the case of the language called 'English' the sheer numbers of English users whose individual performances (and competences) are summated within the fiction of 'English', their worldwide geographical distribution, the great range of social needs and purposes they serve, and the resulting myriad of identifiably different versions of English—all these factors combine to produce a paradox: as English becomes ever more widely used, so it becomes ever more difficult to characterize in ways that support the fiction of a simple, single language.

We must assume that there *is* a link between the diverse manifestations of 'English': in the writings of Chinua Achebe or William Faulkner; in the speech of a taxi driver at Calcutta railway station or a Nigerian professor of economics; in the discourse rules of British diplomatic negotiation or of bar conversation in Nairobi. The link is not fortuitous, but obviously it is highly complex. Being so complex it admits of many alternative modes of analysis. The approach proposed in this book is to view the fiction of 'English' as being manifested in two distinct ways, each having its own separate determining influences. The first of these manifestations of English is social, and we have already considered it in some detail in the previous chapter: English-using communities develop *localized forms of English* (LFEs) which display a profile of numerous variable features. The second manifestation is at the level of the individual user of English, whose command and use of the language is a mixture both of conformity to one or more LFE and at the same time the consequence of specific features in his personal identity.

II. Past views of different forms of English

For over a century and increasingly in recent times it has been commonplace to use labels such as 'Indian English', 'Hong Kong English', 'Australian English', 'West African English', etc. At various times the identity of such notions has been felt to reside in idiosyncrasies of lexis, or syntax, or style; or else it has been ascribed solely to the dimension of accent and dialect; or it has been subsumed within sociolinguistic studies, or to lectal choice, between *acrolect, mesolect,* and *basilect.* Sometimes it has been analysed in terms of 'common errors', i.e. institutionalized inventories of deviations from a presumed norm. Many of these studies have been of great value in illuminating and describing further layers of the onion-skins of language. Most of them have been carried out from a nativist standpoint, i.e. they incorporate an unstated assumption that whatever diversity may occur in the English usage of those for whom English is not the mother tongue, there exists in the usage of the native speaker both a unity and a hierarchical superiority.

It would be naïve to treat this as simple chauvinism and to make the contrary assumption that all Englishes are 'equal' (whatever that means) in every possible sense, including public belief and social prejudice.

Nevertheless, it is necessary to remove value-judgements from consideration and to accept that the language 'English' manifests itself in a large number of forms, that all forms are equally worthy of consideration and potentially acceptable in a given community, and that among the differing characteristics of such forms one must include the native/non-native (L1/L2) dimension.

Some English-using communities require the use of the language, by individuals and in limited numbers, for contact with the external world, for communication with other individuals and communities, for access to science, and the other international uses for which English is the vehicle; these *international* needs constitute the major requirement for English in such countries (e.g. Japan, Turkey, Brazil, etc.). Other English-using communities require the language for these purposes, too, but in addition they need English for *intranational* purposes: for use by large populations within the community. An obvious example of the latter category is India: the great railway system, and the nation's posts, telephones, and telegraphic communications are largely run in English, but by Indians for whom English is not their native language.

As the rather recent result of profound sociolinguistic changes, other countries, notably India and Singapore, arguably Malaysia, in the future doubtless others, also have major international needs for English, even though English is never, in these countries, an indigenous language.

Countries with international needs only for English, and countries with that plus intranational needs, will be referred to as INTER and INTRA types respectively. Thus, those countries in which significant use is made of English although it is an L2 (secondary language, not primary language) for the great majority of the population, are of two kinds: some are INTRA, but some are INTER (i.e. their needs are international only).

In addition, the LFE of INTER-type countries is always *dependent*: it values itself and is valued by others against closeness to an L1 model (i.e. speakers of English in an INTER country seek to approximate to a 'native-speaker' model). INTRA type LFEs, by contrast, while they often express some affinities towards one or another L1 type (e.g. 'Puerto Rican English' has affinities towards American models; 'West African English' has more affinities with British models) are generally *independent*. They do not value themselves directly on closeness to an L1 type, although the educational system may still adhere to former ideas, left over from an era when such sociolinguistic and educational independence was not yet acceptable, either in British or American eyes, or in the country concerned.

It follows from these somewhat complex relationships that the precise values of the set of considerations in determining the analysis and description of LFEs, which were discussed in the previous chapter, namely their defining and differentiating characteristics, are strongly influenced by whether a given LFE is *dependent* upon a native (L1) model or *independent*.

To sum up this section of the argument, whether an LFE is of an IN-TER or INTRA type, its identity will include the precise profile of values of each of the parameters outlined above. These features define the LFE. But in one sense an LFE is as much of a fiction as is the fiction of the language 'English'. No individual speaker/writer of English actually produces in his daily life all or only the LFE of his community. The nature of the LFE is a gross generalization perceived behind and through the idiolectal performance of individuals. They in turn are subject to other influences; it is essential to take these into account because it is their performance which makes up the LFE.

III. Variables reflected in individual performance

The question now arises how we should view the English actually used by an individual. He or she will have been subject to a degree of social pressure, which varies depending on his community and on his personal history, to conform to a localized form of English—or not to do so: perhaps to conform to some other model. This might be called the variable of *personal history*. It applies both to native and non-native speakers, though to differing extents.

But, in addition, the actual performance of the individual may be subject to *shortfall variations*. 'Shortfall' here has the sense of 'not achieving mastery of the acrolect'. Such variations are due to at least three causes.

Shortfall variations

(i) *Incomplete learning.* Particularly for the non-native speaker, it will make a difference how early he got off the English-learning escalator. The difference between the performance of the Calcutta taxi driver and the Delhi professor of zoology is partly a consequence of the latter having spent longer under pressure to conform.

(ii) *Ineffective learning*. Sometimes it is the effectiveness of learning rather than its total duration that has the greatest influence in producing shortfall variations. Ineffectiveness may have its origins in poor teaching, or poor learning, or both.

(iii) *Tacit fossilization*. It is very commonly observed that individuals cease to learn or to acquire a foreign language long before they have reached the presumed limits of their capability to do so. The phenomenon referred to by Selinker, Corder, and others as *fossilization* is often of this kind: the individual decides he can manage his communication needs without further learning, so learning ceases. Or a learner, as part of his growing emotional and social maturity, identifies further language learning with unwelcome social, cultural, or political attitudes, and so he turns off his learning, temporarily or permanently. It often happens that when communication needs change and increase, learning resumes. Most people learn as much or as little of a foreign language as they need, not as much at they are taught. In the case of the localized forms of English, the limited performance of individuals can frequently be ascribed to tacit fossilization, i.e. to an unspoken decision that what he has is sufficient for his needs.

The individual, then, will exhibit his personal set of features, probably within the overall description of the LFE, but certainly not identical to the whole of it. And the nature of his idiolectal performance will be determined by (a) his *personal history,* and (b) his own personal set of *shortfall variations.*

Conclusion

Between the general envelope of 'English', on the one hand, and the actual performance of the individual user of English, on the other hand, we have considered two major concepts. The first is the notion of localized forms of English; these fall into two types according to the needs and purposes of the community, and their description is the sum of a number of sociolinguistic variables. The second concept is that of two main types of variables that influence the individual's actual performance and relate both to his degree of conformity to a localized form of English and to his idiosyncrasy as a member of his English-using community.

Chapter 7

When is a Localized Form of English a Suitable Model for Teaching Purposes?

English is used by an enormous speech-community, probably of 600 million people, of whom about 300 million are speakers of English as their mother tongue, while a further 300 million have learned it in addition to their mother tongue. In considering the world's international languages, what matters is the total community of those who *use* a language, not the smaller population of native speakers. And the larger the total number of users, the larger the number of differentiated versions of the language which will develop within the total envelope of 'English'.

Why is English so widespead, geographically? It is easy to trace the main historical outlines of the spread of English over the world in the eighteenth and nineteenth centuries and to assume that they constitute the reason. But exploration, trade, and conquest are not sufficient by themselves to ensure that a language becomes accepted for use by others as well as by those for whom it is the mother tongue. The Portuguese language illustrates the point: Portuguese, too, was carried across the world in the fifteenth and sixteenth centuries by a dominant European trading nation, and it had the additional impetus of being spread with the crusading fire of the militant Catholic Church. Yet today the Portuguese language, although widely distributed in geographical terms, is used almost solely as the mother tongue of the Portuguese and Brazilian peoples, and hardly at all as a language of international communication by populations of Portuguese L2 users.

Why should English have developed as a language used intensively by other communities when Portuguese has not do so? There are many possible reasons, of which these three may be crucial: (i) English is a *borrowing* language. It has ways of taking the names of ideas and things from other cultures and expressing them in English without native speakers of English feeling that the so-called 'purity' of their language is threatened thereby. (ii) At the same time it possesses a great range of rules for the formation of new words—Appendix I of the *Grammar of Contemporary English* (Quirk, Greenbaum, Leech and Svartvik) contains 56 pages of word-formation. English, it would seem, is well adapted for development and change. (iii) English is the language in which has been principally conducted the genesis of the Second Industrial Revolution.

A complete description of the growth of English in modern times would require more elements than these to be taken into account, but these three may serve to indicate some of the stronger reasons why English today is used by such a vast number of people and comprises such an immense number of different varieties.

In the preceding chapters we have discussed in some detail the emergence of localized forms of English and the ways in which LFEs are different from each other. Here let us consider briefly the fact that some LFEs relate to English native-speaking (L1) communities, and some to English L2 communities.

The form of English used by a given English-using community does not exist in a vacuum: it normally exhibits similarities with other forms of English in the same geographical area, and it displays socio-political affinities with other forms of English. Thus, 'West African English' is obviously more like 'East African English' than, say, Australian English; its sociopolitical affinities are with other independent, black African, English-using communities—and therefore not with, say 'South African English' or 'West Indian English'. At the same time, every form of English aligns decisively with one or other of the two main branches of the English language: British or American.

Together these two types constitute the global family of 'Englishes'; it is possible to construct a 'family tree' of English which roughly illustrates the historical and geographical relationships between them. (Fig. 3)

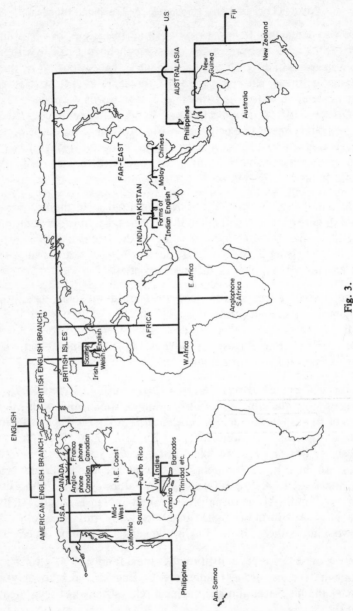

Fig. 3.

As we have seen, some forms of English display larger numbers of identifiable varieties than do others. On the whole, L1 forms possess more varieties than L2 forms; some L2 forms possess near-pidgin varieties which do not occur in L1 forms. The two types of LFEs (L1 and L2) are easier to exemplify than to define. L1 forms would include: Tyneside English; Cockney; Texas English; South Wales English; New South Wales English; West Indies English (with distinctive versions for many individual islands); Tristan da Cunha English; and so forth.

L2 local forms would include: Scottish (Gaelic-speakers') English; West African English; Singapore English; Samoan English; Philippines English; the large numbers of different versions of Indian English; and many more.

Each of the many LFEs consists of that particular constellation of dialect and accent with a particular array of varieties, having affinities with either British or American English, which is current in a given English-using community.

An L1 local form does not normally serve as an educational model. For example, Cockney is not *taught as a model* of English for British children, even in London. Native speakers of English are usually taught how to operate standard—the non-local 'educated' dialect—and how to speak it with an accent that is not so strongly marked that it is unintelligible outside the immediate locality. British children are not normally made to give up their local form of English—though that used to be regarded as a necessary piece of social demolition, half a century ago—but the local form, though tolerated, is not set up as a target to be achieved. If the local form of English is considered at all, it is simply taken for granted as a sort of communally shared base-line.

Such are the educational conventions about what constitutes a suitable educational model in one English L1 country, Britain, at least. They arise from the attitudes of native speakers of English towards their own language and towards the teaching of English for use in their own country.

This is the central issue: criteria of pedagogical models of English are determined by social attitudes towards the language. And there are crucial differences between the attitudes of English L1 communities and those of English L2-using communities. It is time for the ELT profession to recognize these differences, to understand the consequences of these different attitudes, and to accept that they may lead to models of English being used in schools that are unfamiliar in L1 countries.

The great majority of native speakers of English, whether British, American, Australian, New Zealand, or any other, are effectively monolingual (school instruction in foreign languages notwithstanding). They are generally unaware of multilingual conditions: in particular they do not realize that for many millions of people English has become an essential and inherent part of daily life, even though it is not their mother tongue.

In many parts of the world, then, those who use English have attitudes towards their local L2 form of English not greatly different from the attitudes which native speakers have towards their L1 form of English: they take it for granted as part of their corporate cultural identity. But these identities are not the same in the two cases; it is part of the identity of the L2-using community *not* to be the same as the British or the Americans. Language education in a given country, therefore, may need for pragmatic reasons to include English, but the pedagogical model selected for English must reflect local or regional characteristics. It must (a) be mutually intelligible with all other national and international forms, but (b) it must also be different from all others, and (c) recognizably an L2 form, not an L1 form.

We have reached a preliminary answer to the question, When is a local form of English suitable for ELT purposes? The first approximation to an answer is, When a local L2 form exists and is felt by the local speech community to be a desirable form. But two questions remain to be pursued: first, if there is more than one local L2 form, what then is the pedagogical solution? And, second, what if there is *no* local L2 form?

In fact, where a local L2 form exists at all, it exists with several varieties. What can be expected to emerge is not a single form of

English but a scale of 'Englishes' ranging by imperceptibly small differences from, at one extreme, Standard English with some special local vocabulary and expression, spoken with an accent identified with the local educated community, to, at the other extreme, a local dialect, perhaps a local pidgin, with a local and strongly marked accent. English in West and East Africa, for example, find a parallel in Tongue's description of English in Singapore and Malaysia and in Kachru's analysis of the many different kinds of Indian English. It can be seen that in these countries the scale of 'Englishes' relates in broad terms both to levels of educational achievement and to the complexity of the individual's communicative needs. Those who most often require to understand and be understood by English users of another country are almost always those with more education than the average. Those whose needs for communicating in English are fully met by the local near-pidgin are generally those with the least education.

It seems that ELT must aim at a moving target: the further an individual proceeds up the educational scale, the more closely his local L2 form of English needs to conform to standards of international intelligibility. Standards of attainment that are adequate at the lower levels are insufficient at a higher level. As Kachru says ('New Englishes') 'The universality of pedagogical models is suspect: it has to be sacrificed for local sociopolitical, educational, and communicative aims.' There is a difficult problem here: how to identify and teach at each educational level a form of English adequate for the needs at that level, neither insufficient (which would place a burden of deficit upon the individual) nor too sophisticated (which would be a burden on teaching resources). We can be encouraged by the fact that on the whole it happens: standards achieved do roughly match the progression we have been discussing.

Local L2 forms do not develop everywhere. The kinds of distinction we have been making between more strongly differenced and less strongly differenced forms of English are of great importance where such forms exist: elswhere the principles involved are without relevance. The distinction between those areas where L2 forms do exist and those areas where they have not developed is broadly that which is already acknowledged as dividing the 'English as a *Second* Language' (ESL) areas from the English as a *Foreign* Language (EFL) areas.

In EFL areas there exists no local L2 form of English: consequently the most suitable pedagogical model is usually a native-speaker model. In foreign-language teaching generally, the normally accepted target is that of the educated, metropolitan native speaker. Exceptions can occur: Togo provides a possible counter-example. In Togo, English is a *foreign* language, but with Ghana and Nigeria so close, and given the wide public acceptance of West African English, it is not unreasonable if in Togo, too, this ESL form becomes the target even in an EFL country. West African English seems a more suitable target for Togo children than British or American English.

The conclusions to which this analysis leads one are principally these: (i) different models of English are likely to be suitable in EFL areas, as contrasted with ESL areas; (ii) in EFL areas, it is generally appropriate to teach a native-speaker model (British, American, Australian, New Zealand, etc.); (iii) in ESL areas where local L2 forms have developed and where they command public approval it is these forms which constitute the most suitable models for use in schools, certainly more suitable than a British or American L1 model; (iv) the standards of achievement at different levels in the educational system should relate to the expanding communicative requirements of the citizen as he continues his education—the more education he receives, the more widely intelligible in English he should be; and (v) the native speaker of English must accept that English is no longer his possession alone: it belongs to the world, and new forms of English, born of new countries with new communicative needs, should be accepted into the marvellously flexible and adaptable galaxy of 'Englishes' which constitute the English language.

Chapter 8

English for International and Intranational Purposes: A Shift in Linguistic Perspectives

So far in this book we have concentrated on teasing out the new distinctions between the ever-growing localized forms of English, and on trying to illuminate the changing roles and functions required of English by those who use it. One of these new distinctions, that between solely *international* needs and purposes for English (INTER-type LFEs) and needs which are both *international and intranational* (INTRA-type LFEs) has an unusual history. It first emerged into the full consciousness of specialists in English on a specific occasion in 1978. The recognition of the INTER/INTRA distinction was important in itself; but the lessons learned during the process of its birth, so to speak, were also of great importance, and this chapter seeks to explain why that was so.

Most evolutionary processes within professional disciplines change by imperceptible steps, so that at any given moment it is hard even to discern the direction of change, let alone to identify sources of impetus. A conference held in 1978, however, will probably turn out to be an exception to the rule and to have been the occasion of a visible shift in emphasis within the field of the study and teaching of English as a foreign or second language (TEFL). It will at the same time have important consequences for several facets of sociolinguistics, national language planning policy, and descriptive linguistics.

The nature of this shift in emphasis can be simply stated: it is away from an L1-dominated approach and towards an L2-oriented approach to TEFL. That is to say, away from the assumption—usually unstated and often not realized—that 'English' should always be interpreted as 'The English of native speakers of the language', and in the direction of the assumption—already justified by the enormous expansion of English used in communication between non-native speakers—that 'English' also means 'The English of non-native speakers' treated in its own right and accepted on a footing of equality.

Looking back, this present position was doubtless foreshadowed over the past two decades by the acceptance, in British educational circles at least, of terms such as 'educated West African English', 'Singapore English', etc. To admit and accept such labels was to allow implicitly that the English language exists in forms identifiably different from any of those used by native speakers of the language—whether from Great Britain, or North America, or Australia—and that such 'non-native' forms do not have to be rejected out of hand but can be debated and if necessary accepted, on their merits.

Not all scholars and authorities have always accepted this standpoint. Clifford Prator (Prator, 1968) in particular, has argued the exclusively nativist case, taking the line that forms of English emerging in communities of non-native users must inevitably be inferior to L1 forms of English; that since teaching and learning do not constitute a process of high efficiency, the acceptance of a non-native form as the pedagogical target will inevitably lead to progressive deterioration and loss of intelligibility; and that to take a 'permissive' view of local forms of English must be regarded as educational heresy: specifically, the 'British heresy'.

It is perhaps not surprising, in the light of the different historical experience of teaching English as between Britain and the United States, these two opposing views should have grown up. The overwhelming experience of the United States in teaching English as a foreign language has been aimed at the linguistic and cultural assimilation into an English-language nation of indigenous groups and, more especially, of immigrants, having other languages as their mother tongue. The United Kingdom, by contrast, is not an immigration country: its TEFL experience has been overwhelmingly concentrated overseas, on the teaching of children in schools and students in colleges and universities, and on the training of teachers of English. To this end there has grown up a strong network of organizations within Britain which service and act as a source of intellectual development for this predominantly external profession.

There are, of course, many exceptions to these generalizations. The United States has served as the base for numerous major overseas projects for teaching English and for teacher training, while in a few countries—notably the Philippines—the involvement of American professionals in the teaching of English has been broadly similar to (and as long-standing as) the British involvement in countries such as Nigeria or India. It is also the case that a flourishing industry has grown up which provides English-language teaching for overseas learners in Britain. Yet the basic contrast remains at least in terms of the historical development which has helped to shape attitudes towards the Englishes which have developed in various parts of the world. To oversimplify, in America the attitude of teachers has always been 'We are teaching *our* language': in Britain it has often though selectively been 'We are helping them to teach *their* form of our *shared* language'.

It is not irrelevant to the argument of this paper to explain briefly the genesis of the conference in question. The Culture Learning Institute of the East-West Center in Hawaii has for some years included in its programme two courses—one for teacher trainers (of teachers of English) and one for educational administrators (concerned with the teaching of English), designed for professional educationists from Asia, the Far East, and the Pacific Basin. These courses were much appreciated in the countries concerned. However, a policy decision by the governors of the East-West Center that the Center's efforts should not duplicate work done by other institutions, (e.g. American universities) caused the staff of the Culture Learning Institute to consider new and unique ways of making their contribution.

One member of the CLI staff, Mr. Larry Smith, had sensed a change in needs and attitudes among the participants in these courses, towards a concept that he labelled 'English as an international auxiliary language' (EIAL) (Smith, 1980) and it was for the purpose of examining this complex issue, and in order to think it through with the help of specialists from the countries concerned and from the international body of professionals in the field of English studies, that he planned the Hawaii Conference for April 1978.

A number of papers prepared in advance by invited specialists covered such diverse issues as language pragmatics, Indian English, English in Singapore and in Malaysia, the problems of describing local forms of English, attitudes towards English in communities where it is used but is not indigenous, and many other topics. These papers and the intellectual and practical questions which they raised were discussed over a period of 2 weeks, during which a number of crucial issues emerged.

Early in the discussions a terminological and philosophical barrier was encountered, composed of two interlocking parts. In the first place, although the word *auxiliary* was felt by some participants (and had been chosen for this reason) to be neutral and descriptive, and to imply only 'an additional tool', other participants, especially non-native speakers of English, perceived in it a strong sense of 'less than complete', 'inadequate', 'substandard'. It became clear that whatever new concepts were going to emerge they would have to take account of strong feelings engendered in the minds of many overseas users of English that they should not be, as several participants expressed it, 'fobbed off with Mickey Mouse English', or 'chop-suey English'.

Secondly, within the label 'English as an international and auxiliary language' it became clear that the locution 'English as . . .' presupposed the existence, to the minds of many people, of 'an English', i.e. of a degree of reification, of a more or less finite, describable entity, different in some definable respects from other forms of English. This had not been the intention of 'auxiliary' in EIAL. On the contrary, the original concept had been of differing *purposes for* using English rather than different *versions of* the language. The strength of these views and their crucial nature within the argumentation came to the surface in the discussion of closely argued and innovative papers by Quirk (1980) and Stein (1978). The intention of the authors was to suggest that the task of learning English could be made easier for foreign learners by making certain deliberate, rationally motivated simplifications in syntax (Quirk) and lexis (Stein). Yet the initial understanding of some participants was that foreign learners were thus to be offered, by native speakers, a restricted subset of English rather than 'the whole of' the language. In actual practice, as every teacher of a foreign language is aware, during the early stages of language courses restrictions *are* made, complicated systems *are* avoided until later, vocabulary selection *is* carried out. What Quirk's proposal for 'nuclear English' provides, almost for the first time, is a firmly based rationale for deciding which restrictions and selections to make, and for describing a 'way-stage' for the learner. In the context of the Hawaii Conference it was illuminating to observe the unexpected differences of emotive interpretation that become attached to apparently neutral, objective contributions to the debate. The lesson is that statements about language simplification, which are acceptable within the framework of language pedagogy, may be unacceptable unless given further exegesis when extrapolated to a framework of national language policy.

It took several days for these fundamental distinctions to be assimilated. While this was going on, a further crux was identified and discussed, namely, between two different types of use of English among non-native users, and, following from this difference, between two types of national outlook on English. On the one hand, papers by Kachru (1980a) and by Willard Shaw (1980) brought forward evidence from India and elsewhere in South-east Asia, of strikingly large numbers of people, not being native speakers of English, for whom the use of English is normal and essential. It was reported that in India some 29 million people use English as a matter of course, for example. Further, the English used by people in this situation is not felt to be relatable to (i.e. valued by measuring variations from) the English of native speakers, whether from Britain, North America, Australasia, or elsewhere. On the other hand, participants from Japan, Afghanistan, and some other countries expressed the view that for them English was also a valuable tool of communication, that it is used by virtually nobody as a normal vehicle of daily discourse, and that its use by their compatriots was, indeed, to be evaluated by reference to a native-speaker model.

One might at first think that this was simply the *foreign language/second language* distinction reappearing in a different guise. But during the discussion of these issues two further points became clear. Firstly, the ESL/EFL distinction related to the universe of discourse of language teaching, but it is not adequate in the analysis of national uses of, and purposes for, particular languages. Secondly, SL/FL tend to be regarded as either/or distinctions, whereas it is necessary to be able to allow for circumstances in which an infinite gradation of mixtures of the one and the other type is present.

The terms eventually accepted were based upon the *purposes* for which English is used in a given community (not even in a given nation: it was reported that within India some States show a very different profile of purposes from other States). These were distinguished as *international* and *intranational* purposes as we have differentiated them in preceding chapters. (The more familar terms *external* and *internal* were considered, but most participants felt that the semantic flavour of 'nation' was desirable, and perhaps that the punning alternative meaning of *international* as 'among our nationals', in addition to the more obvious 'within the nation', made the pair *international/intranational* more appropriate.)

This particular crux, then, concerned the purposes and uses of English, and its elucidation was taken one stage further. Examples of countries (within the purview of this conference) where the purposes of English were solely or predominantly *international,* include the following: Japan, Indonesia, China, etc. Countries whose purposes for English include a serious *intranational* component, include: India, Pakistan, Malaysia, Singapore, Hong Kong, Sri Lanka, Papua New Guinea, and most Pacific countries. etc.

What was in fact being said was that where there are *intranational purposes* for English, a form of English develops which has identifiable characteristics and forms a recognizable element of cultural identity for those who share it. Two different observations need to be made. Firstly, these latter communities have international purposes, too, not solely intranational ones. In other words, English serves international purposes in a great many communities where it is not the mother tongue, and intranational purposes in some of them. When the purposes are international *only,* no special, local form of English merges, and the standards used for evaluating command of English (including an educational model) are normally transferred from an English-speaking country; when the purposes include intranational ones in addition to international ones, a local form of English develops which serves both sets of purposes and is not transferred from native-speaker models.

The second observation is that, generally speaking, English for international purposes is needed and exercised by *individuals*; English for intranational purposes is needed and exercised by *populations*. This is not simply a statement of numerical scale: it relates also to social attitudes. If we refer to them for convenience as INTER countries (international purposes only) and INTRA countries (with a major element of intranational purposes) respectively, in INTER countries or communities command of English, to whatever level, is achieved on an individual basis for study or occupational needs and the individuals are in a small minority, whereas in INTRA countries there exists a local form of English, command of which it is taken as normal for a sizeable proportion of citizens to achieve. These differences can have profound consequences for the provision and organization of foreign-language education, and, indeed, it is to a large extent the understanding of this consequential relationship which constitutes the most important outcome of the Hawaii Conference.

The consequences of this distinction, for linguistic description and for pedagogical principle are considerable. As to description, INTER forms (i.e. identifiable forms of English employed in communities where English is used solely for international purposes) aim at a more or less close approximation to native-speaker English—typically, at Standard English, spoken with a British, North-American, or Australasian accent. Observable and systematic variations from the native-speaker model are of three main kinds: (i) *special local usages,* either relating to fauna, flora, topography, or institutions having no exact counterpart in native-speaker English (as when a Japanese refers to the 'Diet', in the absence of any translation equivalent and in order to avoid the inappropriate 'House of Commons'); (ii) *shortfall varia-*

tions, caused either by incomplete learning (e.g. by the pupil who leaves school at 14 before completing the 'full' course of instruction which he might have followed), or by ineffective learning (e.g. through poor teaching or poor performance as a pupil), or by tacit fossilization (e.g. by the individual having decided that he has learned sufficient for his personal requirements and so ceasing to learn further); and (iii) *interference variation,* stemming from incomplete change from one set of linguistic, semantic, and cultural patterns to another (e.g. foreign accent). In any given community these three types of observable variation are sufficiently systematic to be easily identified with that community. Nevertheless, in describing and rationalizing the causes of all these variations within INTER forms of English, the frame of reference is that of a native speaker model.

INTRA forms, however, merit description on a more complex basis. It is possible to distinguish two sets of variables, one of which defines any given local INTRA forms of English (e.g. 'Indian English', 'Singapore English', etc), while the other set distinguishes between different LFEs.

A further difference between INTER and INTRA types of LFE is that the latter (e.g. Indian English) exhibit variation along a scale of 'markedness'. This is often referred to through the use of the terms *acrolect, mesolect,* and *basilect,* which roughly conflate concepts of precise versus not precise, formal versus informal, slang-free versus slang-using, higher social class versus lower social class. What has often confused native-speaker observers of INTRA types of English is the easy and frequent lect-switching which they observe. Thus an educated professional person (for example) in India will at one moment be discussing with a UK visitor the teaching of English, using Standard English with an accent that displays virtually no evidence of local affiliation; an educated neighbour arrives, and the two local people converse in Indian English, i.e. an INTRA LFE, but in its acrolectal form; a few minutes later, the laundry is delivered, and the discourse at once switches to the most-marked, basilectal Indian LFE, in the form of a pidgin. Monolingual, mono-dialectal British or American observers are often disturbed by this ease of switching.

Towards the end of the Hawaii Conference an attempt was made to summarize the common ground of concepts and belief that had come to be shared by the participants. All were agreed that acceptance of the INTER/INTRA distinction logically required a reappraisal of academic and educational attitudes and programmes in all countries where the use of English is a major activity. Specifically, the participants outlined new needs under four headings: (a) basic research, (b) applied research, (c) documentation, dissemination, and liaison, (d) professional support activities. Thus they recognized that the fundamental distinctions and conceptualizations which they had been elucidating had consequences far wider than those normally admitted into the discussion of the teaching of English.

In retrospect, the Hawaii Conference can be interpreted as giving force and importance—through the distinction of the participants and the depth and intensity of their discussions—to a number of propositions: that the English language must be accepted as not simply or solely the cultural possession of those who are its native speakers but also the possession of great populations of users for whom it is a foreign language; that a crucial distinction is required between communities for whom English serves international purposes only and those for whom intranational purposes are essential; that attitudes towards 'Indian English', 'Malaysian English', etc., need to be revised in the light of this distinction; that accordingly the identification and establishment of educational targets, and the assessment of achievement in English, needs radical adjustment; that a new impetus has been given, together with a changed direction, to basic and applied research programmes concerned with language planning and English-language teaching; that the type of assistance that it will in future be most appropriate for native English-speaking countries to offer in the field of English language will be different in INTRA countries from that which is most helpful in INTER countries; and that in INTRA countries it may not be so much as direct teachers of English that native speakers can in future make their biggest contribution, but at a more sophisticated level, e.g. as higher-level specialists in applied linguistics and generally in helping these countries to handle for themselves the subtle and complex problems which these new attitudes will engender.

Appendix I. Suggestions proposed by the Conference on English as an international auxiliary language held from 1-15 April 1978 at the East-West Center, Hawaii

1. As professionals, members of the conference felt that the stimulus given to the question of English used as an international or auxiliary language has led to the emergence of sharp and important issues that are in urgent need of investigation and action.

2. These issues are seen as summarized in the distinction between the uses of English for international (i.e. external) and intranational (i.e. internal) purposes.[1] This distinction recognizes that, while the teaching of English should reflect in all cases the sociocultural contexts and the educational policies of the countries concerned, there is a need to distinguish between (a) those countries (e.g. Japan) whose requirements focus upon international comprehensibility, and (b) those countries (e.g. India) that, in addition, must take account of English as it is used for their own intranational purposes. This distinction need not, of course, supersede the useful terms 'foreign language' and 'second language', but provides a broader perspective within which we can view the dynamics of the language situation of a wide range of countries.

3. So far as we know, no organization exists that takes account of any language in the light of this fundamental distinction, and we congratulate the East-West Center on having provided the initial thinking that has led to its recognition. The Culture Learning Institute constitutes a very good base for embarking on activities in this area.

4. It is not for us to define or prescribe the policies to be adopted, but the papers and discussions at the conference have identified a number of fundamental issues. These issues can be considered under four headings:

    (a) Basic research.
    (b) Applied research.

---

[1] At the beginning of the conference, 'auxilary' was used in the sense proposed by the Culture Learning Institute as a language used within a country. In the course of the conference it was found that the term can be misinterpreted, and it was replaced by 'intranational'.

(c) Documentation, dissemination, and liaison.

(d) Professional support activities.

5. *Basic research*: e.g. descriptive and empirical studies of English in different settings; fact-finding (supported by relevant statistics) at international, national, regional, and local levels, in relation to roles, functions, attitudes, expectations, achievement, etc.; studies in the feasibility of devising a core English for international use; development of research techniques appropriate to such investigations as those listed above.

6. *Applied research*: e.g. studies of the implications of the international-intranational distinction of language learning/teaching; arising from such studies, the elaboration of a framework of concepts and data, leading first to a reappraisal of goals, approaches, methods, materials, tests, examinations, and teacher training, and subsequently to the necessary curriculum development with appropriate modes of evaluation.

7. *Documentation, dissemination, and liaison*: e.g. promoting and creating resource centres for descriptive linguistic data and acting as a clearing house for the results of such other research as listed in 5 and 6; the interpretation and dissemination of research findings and other relevant information appropriate to specific countries and regions; liaison with relevant institutions, organizations, and professional associations.

8. *Professional support activities*: the understanding of the findings and consequences of the foregoing research and development activities will require the institution of a well co-ordinated programme of workshops and conferences as well as advisory and training programmes. These would focus upon particular intranational, international, and professional questions, and should be organized with flexibility in the choice of location. Meetings should have two crucial aims: (a) assisting in professionalizing a teaching force, and (b) enabling policy-makers and administrators to become familiar with all these developments and to elaborate ways of implementing them in their situations. Future support activities will need increasingly to reflect the new orientation that has emerged.

Part III

TEACHING ENGLISH FOR SCIENTIFIC AND OTHER SPECIFIC PURPOSES

Chapter 9
'Functional Englishes' (ESP)

Introduction

In this chapter we shall seek to categorize the major and rapidly developing branch of English-language teaching usually called ESP (English for specific purposes). In Britain a remarkable feature of this development is the close relation between theory, on the one hand (especially *applied linguistics,* defined roughly as 'a multidisciplinary approach to the solution of language-based problems' (Strevens, 1978a)), and practical classroom needs, on the other.

'Functional English' as a response to geo-linguistic changes

Within the general context of the recent and massive global expansion of the use of English (Fishman *et al.,* 1977; Kachru, 1965-80 inclusive, Smith, 1980; Strevens, 1978a, 1978b, 1979, 1979) there has occurred during the same period a great increase in the demand for instruction in English as a foreign language. It is striking to observe that this demand is less and less generalized in its nature and more and more closely related to the learners' needs and wishes. Thus where in 1970 the great majority of EFL was provided as 'general English' in the form of 'English as a subject of a liberal arts education', in 1980 this generalized EFL Provision is declining in many countries at the same time as there is building up a more-than-proportionate increase in demand for and provision of 'functional Englishes' or ESP.

The reasons for this expansion of demand and the consequent evolution of its nature are complex, but they include at least the following:

(i) The separation, in the estimation of many communities of users of English, of the English language as a valuable instrument (which has come to be regarded as a local, national, and international asset) from the set of cultural values associated with native speakers of English (notably (a) the domestic, family, and social life of the British or

Americans as evidenced in the great majority of teaching courses, and (b) English literature, (especially when presented as embodying a set of superior moral values), i.e. they want and accept the instrument as long as they are not required to swallow the gall of an alien culture and society.

(ii) The range of sociolinguistic pressures associated with newly-won political independence and nationhood, when these arise in multilingual societies simultaneously with urgent needs for economic development.

(iii) The emergence in many countries of 'localized forms of English' as detailed in Part II of this book, competence in which is measured against locally felt communicative needs and not against the norms of native speakers of English, whether British, American, Australian, or other.

(iv) A 'backlash' in some newly independent societies against the incursion of English into certain cultural domains, to the detriment of local cultural pride, cohesion, or expressions, particularly where instruction in English at primary school level has been permitted to 'crowd out' instruction in the native languages.

(v) As a consequence of (iv) above, in some countries a more selective acceptance of English, resisting its use for the earliest years of education and for the discussion of local cultural ideas, but licensing it, so to speak, for use in specific but restricted areas: these areas include not only science and 'econo-technics' (Fishman *et al.,* 1977) but also the various trains of international activity for which English serves as a vehicle: the mass media of information and entertainment including films, radio, and TV; international aid and administration; pop music; marketing and advertisement by multinational corporations; literature written in English by non-native speakers of English, etc.

It is against this background that the current growth in demand for functional English can be set; however, the existence of this demand has not been universally recognized by the teaching profession of English as a foreign language. A sizeable (though diminishing) sector of the profession, trained in the humanistic tradition, convinced of the superordinate value of English literature as the ultimate justification for learning and teaching English, convinced that departure from native-speaker norms and models will loosen the knot of international intelligibility that binds the English language together, and unwilling (in business terms) to modify the product which they supply in spite of major changes in the nature of the market demand—this section of the profession continues to work broadly as it has done for over 25 years.[1]

What we are here concerned with, then, is that large and growing sector of EFL that, recognizing a major change in the demand for English, has modified its ideas and procedures in order to meet this demand and so to provide instruction in direct response to learners' needs. In one respect this modification has the impetus and sanction of a worldwide trend towards 'learner-centred education' in all subjects; in other ways it is a response to particular requirements, and that response has been strongly shaped by certain lines of intellectual inquiry and commitment in the field of language learning and teaching.

Intellectual sources in ESP

In successful practice, ESP shares with all other branches of foreign-language learning and teaching the fundamental qualities of a skilled teacher cherishing a willing learner (see Chapter 2.) In ESP the skills required of the teacher are, of course, moulded and supported by sound pedagogy and sophisticated methodology, but additionally and integrally—and there lies the difference—by relevant and highly specific principles derived from a range of evolving theoretical and intellectual developments. Since all teachers know of, or pay lip-service to, a dimly perceived relation between 'theory' at some remote level and 'practice' in the classroom, it is important to insist that in the brief but speedy evolution of ESP there has been a rare and close integration of these two aspects. In Britain at least, the sudden establishment of teaching courses in ESP and the production of a mass of specialized

[1] Its contribution is, of course, of great value. No criticism is here being made of competence; indeed, the very conditions of present change are partly the consequence of three decades of dedicated and rather successful English-language teaching within the 'general English' framework. But the times are a-changing.

materials for practical teaching has been led in most cases by individuals or teams working simultaneously on a range of theoretical questions within the broad field of applied linguistics. These questions, which are discussed in greater detail in a subsequent section, may be summarized as follows:

(i) issues in learner-centred instruction and individualization, drawing on educational theory;
(ii) schemata for the analysis of learners' needs;
(iii) the study of discoursal rules, rhetoric analysis, and the categorization of communicative capabilities;
(iv) the nexus of ideas covered by the labels 'notional-functional-communicative';
(v) systems for cross-linguistic equivalence in language instruction;
(vi) principles of syllabus design;
(vii) rationales for the production of teaching materials.

ESP: definition and analysis

English for specific purposes contrasts with 'general English' (often cynically referred to as 'English for the exam'), but the nature of ESP rests rather on the ends to which the English is put and the needs of the learner who experiences those needs. It always requires the appropriate selection of language content (e.g. 'the language of tropical agriculture'; 'the language of electrical power transmission engineering', etc.)—including not solely lexical and grammatical items but also rhetorical and communicative capabilities—and it sometimes requires restriction of the language skills to be learned; e.g. 'within the field of low-temperature physics, a reading-only knowledge'; 'over VHF radio circuits, a recognition knowledge solely of spoken numbers'; 'in the field of meteorology, the ability to understand spoken met. data and to read written text, but on the productive side, merely the ability to type this information on to a teleprinter'; etc.

The following is offered as a working definition of ESP:
'ESP entails the provision of English language instruction:

(i)   devised to meet the learner's particular needs;

(ii) related in themes and topics to designated occupations or areas of study;

(iii) selective (i.e. 'not general') as to language content;

(iv) when indicated, restricted as to the language "skills" included.'

It will be seen that a definition of ESP that is both simple and watertight is not easy to produce. In support of the above working definition we offer here an outline of the principal stages of task-analysis which need to be followed in determining a particular ESP requirement and in approaching the design of a learning/teaching programme for that requirement.

Stage 1: A detailed analysis of the learner's needs, starting from the standpoint that it is not 'general English' that is needed, and that the learner (or his sponsors) can supply comprehensive information about the aims, purposes, needs, wants, roles, functions, etc., for which English is required in his or her circumstances.

Stage 2: Determination of the extent of scientific/technical content. Some ESP requirements (but by no means all, and to a varying extent) make use of 'the English of science' as outlined in Chapter 10. This constitutes an additional element to be learned, with a number of features of its own.

One of the common problems of ESP is that the learners may be familiar with 'the language of science' in their own language, but the teachers of English are not. The teachers often feel, erroneously, that they are required to become as capable of initiating scientific discourse in English as their pupils already are in another language. In practice, however, it is far more important that the teachers should recognize the importance of the rhetorical, discoursal, and communicative features of scientific English, and that they should bend themselves to helping such learners to express the purposes and roles of being a scientist rather than that the teacher should address himself to the apparently obvious yet ultimately trivial task of teaching scientific terminology—much of which turns out to be already known or easily guessable.

Stage 3: Determination whether needs are 'educational' or 'occupational'. With few exceptions, ESP is required for purposes either of *study* or of *work*. These categories are not watertight: language instruction may be part of a period of study that falls within the longer time-scale of a working career—as when French tanker captains are brought ashore for courses in modern radar, electronics, and communications, and find that English forms a major element in the course. Nevertheless, teachers of ESP commonly find that their learners lean principally towards one or other of these polarities: they are typically either (a) students of a particular subject, learning it in English or with English as a component of their studies, or students requiring 'study skills' in English (the ability to understand lectures given in English, to read extensively and therefore rapidly in English, to make notes or take down references in English, to write essays or describe experimental results in English, above all to write examinations in English) prior to starting a course of study in higher education; or (b) people already in an occupation who now need to learn English for use in that occupation (e.g. foreign doctors wishing to practise medicine in Britain).

Stage 4: Determination whether instruction in English precedes educational/occupational training, or follows it, or is concurrent with it. The importance of this question lies in its effects on (a) motivation and willingness to learn (b) the attitudes of the learner towards his teachers, and, above all, (c) the breadth of the conceptual gulf between learner and teacher.

As to (a), an individual who is deeply engaged, full-time, in studying a subject or in training intensively for a particular job, commonly fails to appreciate the ultimate need he will have for an appropriate command of English. This is true for most subjects—chemistry, accountancy, tropical agriculture, etc.—and for most occupations—policeman, architect, pharmacist, plant-breeder, etc. But there are exceptions: the hotel and tourist trades, aviation, and (increasingly) seafaring are occupations where many lines of personal advancement absolutely require some command of English. But they remain exceptions to the general rule. Thus, 'English for engineering students' is typically regarded as a formality, a nuisance, a waste of time. Attention tends to be poor and results likewise. Part of the ESP task is to overcome these negative attitudes. By contrast, the ESP learner whose study and training lie behind him generally knows that he needs English and for what purposes.

As to (b), post-experience and post-training students (i.e. learners of English who are already specialists in a subject or a job) tend to be of relatively mature years and with a personal history of reasonably successful learning behind them—often long behind them. Such learners may find it difficult to return to the role of student, may dislike being taught by teachers much younger than themselves, and may resent the teaching if it does not correspond in pedagogical form to memories of their earlier education. The attitude may be summed up thus: 'All right, young woman. I suppose you must know *something*. I'm sitting down facing you. Now *teach* me!' Again, part of the ESP task is to allay fears, reverse hostile attitudes, achieve mutual confidence (Currie, Sturtridge, and Allwright, 1972).

As to (c), the conceptual gulf between the mature learner and the ESP teacher often seems wide from both sides. The learner is quick to notice any lack of authenticity in the teaching materials, and if he does so, may feel sufficiently wounded in his professional self-esteem (already bruised by 'returning to school') to suspend or abandon his learning of English. The teacher of ESP is invariably and acutely conscious of *not* being a specialist in the learner's subject or occupation. When a teacher of English as a foreign language first embarks on teaching ESP it is generally many months before he or she ceases to be haunted at every lesson by the fear of 'making a mistake in the subject' or even simply of 'not understanding the texts'. The ESP task requires teachers to accept from the outset that they will never be specialists in the learners' subjects—but they also have to learn that *this does not matter*: the task is a three-way partnership in which the teacher first seeks the assistance of a subject specialist, for the purpose of preparing suitable English-teaching materials, and then helps the learner to become able to operate within his own role and identity as a specialist in English. ESP teachers are not normally teachers of specialist subjects (except in rare and fortunate cases) and they should not attempt to be so.

Stage 5: Preparation of suitable syllabuses and teaching materials. In principle every ESP learner or group of learners has its own identifying profile of needs and purposes and therefore requires its own individual syllabus, its own range of teaching materials, its own appropriate methodology. In practice there is a good deal of overlap and partial similarity. Thus a syllabus and materials especially prepared for a particular group (say, Saudi Arabian pharmacists) will, if successful, attract further similar groups, and perhaps also pharmacists from the United Arab Emirates; the mathematical content of navigation courses in English for Japanese airline pilots has some overlap with navigation courses in English for French ships' officers; learners whose mother tongue is Arabic will all have similar learning problems in reading and writing, regardless of their speciality; and so forth.

But the principle is fundamental: ESP is based on a close analysis of the learner's needs. And this has important consequences, since it requires the necessary professional competence in syllabus design and materials production to be applied by those responsible for the teaching, in every case. This is a very different position from 'general English', where syllabuses (usually, alas, determined by a hallowed examination) differ little from each other, are usually unchanged over many years, and do not vary according to the learner's needs (except in broad ways such as age group and level of educational institution). To meet these unvarying conditions the principal thrust of teacher education has been to produce competent classroom practitioners, capable of maximizing the learning success of the learners within a given and invariate syllabus, and using a range of already existing, commercially published teaching materials. Only a very few teachers found themselves required to take part in syllabus design, or engaged in materials writing, and these were the more experienced, better-trained, higher-qualified teachers. Yet for ESP these high-level activities are needed frequently. In consequence, there has been a rapid drive in the provision of further training (commonly by a one-year, course-work MA in applied linguistics, or similar title), while numbers of teachers not thus qualified have found themselves pitched into higher-level professional tasks unprepared. Many have survived through merit and intelligence: a recent feature of ESP is the emergence of a number of excellent and expert practitioners as a result of unsought experience. In a few cases, the outcome has been less effective than was required, or even disastrously bad, but by and large ESP has shown that the EFL profession in Britain possesses great strength and flexibility, and much latent professional talent has been brought forward. The development of ESP has led to a spate of new syllabuses and of materials, both published and unpublished. There have also been written a remarkable quantity of theoretical, theoretical-practical, and practical articles on ESP syllabuses and materials, since c 1977. (See Kennedy, 1978; Hawkey, 1978; Holden, 1977; also the bibliographical references in Strevens, 1978c, and Cowan, 1977.)

Main theoretical lines of emphasis

This chapter is concerned more with theoretical than with practical issues: in this section we comment in turn on each of the eight areas identified in stage 3 above as constituting the principal intellectual lines of emphasis contributing to current work in ESP.

(i) *Learner-centred instruction and individualization*

It is noteworthy that much of the ESP development in Britain takes place in university departments having commitments not only to applied linguistics, as mentioned above, but also to the initial and further training of teachers. Consequently developments in educational theory, in this instance the trend towards learner-centred instruction, can be expected to colour ESP work. Nevertheless, it is probably true that advances in individualization and personalized instruction have come to be made more rapidly in the United States than in Britain, while conversely it is in Britain that ESP has the longest history of development. Workers in both countries are now in close and frequent touch, and largely as a result, the potentialities of personalized instruction are now being explored in Britain also (Altman and James, 1980).

(ii) *Analysis of learners' needs*

Three different lines of approach can be distinguished:

(a) *Development of a theoretical framework of needs-analysis*: notably in the work of Munby (1978), whose direct approach to the categorization of linguistic and communicative behaviours goes beyond that of Richterich and Chancerel (1977, republished 1980) and Bung (1973, republished 1980) and perhaps—although it is of considerable intellectual importance and of seminal influence—reaches the limit of what is practically useful.

(b) *Pragmatic analyses*: several teams, especially those associated with Candlin, Sinclair, Widdowson, and Wilkins, faced with specific types of learners, have undertaken the observation, collection, recording, transcription, and analysis of actual behaviours (e.g. of doctor-patient conversations (Candlin *et al.* 1978a, and b) and of teacher-pupil classroom discourse (Sinclair and Coulthard, 1975)) and have elucidated therefrom a number of principles at a high level of generality and consonant with several lines of current linguistic theory.

(c) *The systems approach* of Trim, van Ek, and the Council of Europe project (discussed further below) in which the schemata devised by Richterich and Bung have been adapted in order to select a particular population of language learners with specified communicative needs for which the threshold level specifications (in English, French, Spanish, German, etc.) have subsequently been precisely drawn up.

(iii) *Categorization of communicative capabilities*[1]

Concurrently with a problem-oriented approach to learners' needs most of the same researchers are engaged in the study of rhetorical structures in spoken and written text and of discoursal rules. The object is to arrive at categories of communicative capability (examples: (a) e.g. GREET, ELICIT, INTERROGATE, QUESTION, MAKESURE, EXTEND, ACTION-INFORM, etc. (from Candlin, Bruton, and Leather, 1974, 1976:—NB:—these are only 7 of their 23 'functions'); (b) in a specific instance of *problem identification: ascription* of properties, *exemplification* of properties, *differentiation, justification* of the differentiation (Jones 1975, quoted in

---

[1]The terms 'communicative competence' is deliberately avoided here as belonging to the cognate but separate universe of discourse of linguistics.

Candlin 1979); (c) communicative categories observed within a factory: (1) *General*: instructions, questions, seeking advice, stating difficulties or objections, suggesting alternatives, measurements and quantities, dangers and emergencies, injury, and health, etc.: (2) *Social communication*: face-to-face conversation and social writing, receiving and making telephone calls; (3) *Special communicative purposes* (various) (in Strevens, 1977b, 1978a). It is important to state, first, that the sets of categories towards which such studies are moving are intended to be both descriptively and theoretically defensible; and, second, that frequent reference is made in the British applied linguistic literature to American work in ethnomethodology and speech-act linguistics, which accords well with the thread of Hallidayan and neo-Firthian systemic linguistics that is to be found throughout this work on communicative capabilities.

(iv) *'Notional'-'functional'-'communicative' ideas*

These three terms are currently frequent in occurrence in applied linguistics and in language teaching, not only in relation to ESP. They are to be encountered separately and also in compounds: 'notional/functional', 'communicative functions', 'communicative notions', etc. The multiple usages reflect uncertainty as to precise meanings on the part of many of those who use the terms—and these include textbook writers, publishers, and educational administrators, not all of whom are aware of these terms in their more original and restricted meanings.

Concentrating here on their relevance to ESP, these terms jointly reflect an attitude towards language: an attitude that concerns itself with the expression of ideas, with rhetorical and discoursal aspects, with speech or writing as directed to meaningful contact between human beings. This contrasts with attitudes towards language that see it as essentially a collection of listable linguistic entities: grammatical rules, lexical items, paradigms, etc.

The term 'notions' in the context of ESP is strongly associated with work by Wilkins towards the Council of Europe project. His original working paper (Wilkins, 1973: its influence has been great, in directions that were not indicated by its rather opaque title) and his subsequent book (Wilkins, 1976) presented to many people for the first time the possibility of describing, at a new and higher level of generality, that which learners need to learn and hence which teachers need to teach. To take a trivial example, the need to learn/teach the following: *o'clock, numbers 1-12, at x o'clock, now, midnight, days of the week, months of the year, dates, seasons,* etc, can all be referred to as 'point of time', a subsection of the notion TIME. Other notions include PLACE, QUANTITY, CASE (in the Fillmore sense of 'who does what, who to, and with what results') and several others.

'Function' in the usages here referred to has strong associations (acknowledged by Wilkins, though he also stresses differences) with Halliday's three basic functions of language: *ideational, textual, interpersonal* (Halliday, 1973, 1978). The kinds of 'function' commonly cited in ESP literature are: *describing, questioning, apologizing, socializing, refusing something offered, praising, criticizing,* etc.

'Communicative', as a term in this N-F-C set, overlaps considerably with 'function' and 'functional', except that there is a greater concentration on the person-to-person intent, and upon the desire of a human being for effective interaction, through speech or writing, with another human being.

As a mnemonic device rather than a definition, the three terms may be categorized thus:

> NOTIONS about the universe
> FUNCTIONS of language
> COMMUNICATION between people

To sum up, the current intensive study among applied linguists of N-F-C aspects of language links in one direction with theory and in another direction with practical language-teaching programmes, including almost all those which may be labelled ESP.

(v) *Systems for cross-linguistic equivalence in the learning and teaching of languages.*
The brief discussion of 'notional' ideas in the preceding subsection forms only part of a major programme of research and development

being carried out under the auspices of the Council of Europe by a multinational team led by J. L. Trim (Trim *et al* 1980). Their long-term aim is the improvement of communication among European nationals by facilitating easier and more effective language learning: this facilitation is based on comprehensive analyses of the learning tasks; it is intended to lead to mutual recognition of language-learning steps of achievement through a unit/credit teaching system; and to this latter end it specifies what is to be learned for a given level in terms which are general to any language and are then defined therefrom in a detailed specification for a given language. The first results of this research are centred on an initial or 'threshold' level (roughly, a level of attainment below which it would barely be worth the learner starting to learn the language, but which forms an adequate basis for further learning, whether by self-study methods or through institutionalized means). The language and communication needs of a particular group of learners has been selected (adults travelling in Europe for work or pleasure having fairly superficial communicative needs and purposes); following a sophisticated investigation of needs-analysis and the elaboration of notional, functional, and communicative categories (Richterich, Bung, Wilkins, op.cit,), 'threshold-level specifications' are now being prepared which state in comprehensive detail for each specific language the realizations in that language of the generalized specification. For example, under *TIME: Point of Time,* the specification for English will include: *at 7 o'clock, in 10 minutes' time, next Wednesday,* etc.; for French: *à 7 heures, dans 10 minutes, mercredi prochain,* etc.; for German: *um 7 Uhr, nach 10 Minuten, nächsten Mittwoch,* etc. (Trim, 1978; van Ek, 1977; Coste 1976). The T-level specification is not, of course, a syllabus, still less a methodology: it is a detailed specification of what one closely specified category of learners requires to be able to do with a foreign language, and what the language is that he needs to do it with. There are signs already that the careful and intelligent approach to the problems involved, the attraction of practical instructional tools based on clearly stated principles, which in turn rest on a coherent theoretical basis—that these qualities will lead to elaborations for school and institutional uses including 'general English' and their adoption as standard practice in many European countries. When that happens, it will represent the converse of past practice: instead of beginning from 'general English' and then devising ad hoc ESP materials, it will be starting from a needs-analysis, 'functional English', or ESP approach and subsequently revising this for more general use.

(vi) *Principles of syllabus design*

It will be realized that language teaching in Britain is basically interventionist in the sense that experience and principle both indicate the possibility of improving learning by the deliberate design of teaching. The establishment of a syllabus (American English: *curriculum*) has in modern times been a chief instrument in the planning of language teaching at least since the 1920s, when the practical classroom difficulties of direct method teaching forced upon teachers the need to formalize in advance the content and sequence of what they sought to teach. Principles for syllabus design have evolved since then, largely by the addition of further criteria to be allowed for in ever-increasing complexity of control. Thus 'linguistic' criteria[1] were followed by 'situational' criteria, and more recently by 'notional', 'functional' and 'communicative' criteria. As far as ESP is concerned, the primacy of needs-analysis reinforces the role of the syllabus in establishing the 'what' and 'when' of teaching (which, incidentally, does not presuppose a rigorous sequence: 'when' can mean 'whenever . . .' as well as 'X after Y but before Z'). It it not surprising that many of those working in the main British centres of ESP development have concerned themselves directly with syllabus design (Johnson, 1976; Morrow and Johnson, 1976, Munby, 1978; Shaw, 1975; Strevens, 1978c).

(vii) *Rationales for the production of teaching materials*

As the complexity of ESP increases, so attempts are constantly being made to find or produce countervailing simplicity. One illustration of

---

[1]In both senses: (a) *linguistic* from 'language', where the principle was mainly lexical and grammatical selection and grading (e.g. in the tradition represented by Sweet, Jespersen, Palmer, Hornby, Mackin, etc.); (b) *linguistic* from 'linguistics', where the principle was the deliberate following of a linguistic theory (e.g. in the audiolingual tradition of Fries, Lado, Marckwardt, etc., and the 'anti-audiolingual' school of Rutherford and Diller). Traditions (a) and (b) constitute the characteristic approaches of British and American EFL teaching respectively, though there are exceptions on both sides.

this is to be found in the area of teaching materials for ESP, where sets of principles are under development such that maximum use is made of previous experience and of adaptation from earlier uses, and the need to start from scratch with each new set of learners is kept to the minimum. A good example is in Donovan (1978), where a single course-book is intended to help all those—learners and teachers alike—whose needs include the language of basic science.

The claims made for ESP and the costs of achieving them

The claims made for ESP, overtly or tacitly, rest on the following central assumptions:

(i) that time and effort will be expended only on that which the learner will need;

(ii) conversely, that no time and effort will be wasted on irrelevant matters;

(iii) that, in consequence, the learning of the target material will be more rapidly achieved;

(iv) that morale, motivation, and willingness to learn will be higher than with 'general English';

(v) that success rates will also be higher;

(vi) that both learner-satisfaction and (not unimportantly) teacher-satisfaction will be higher;

(vii) that in logistic terms a given expenditure on English-language education, channelled through ESP, will be more cost-effective than the same effort channelled solely through 'general English'.

It is the common experience of the past decade that these claims *can* in practice be substantiated—but are not inevitably so. Against the impressive list of benefits claimed for ESP there must be set a number of countervailing costs, or rather, prerequisites for success. These are:

(i) *ESP requires superior teachers.* Not all those who are good teachers of 'general English' will be good teachers of ESP. The teaching force for ESP needs to be capable not only of classroom presentation but of full participation in syllabus design, materials production, test construction, fruitful collaboration with subject specialists, and methodological innovation. Hence, compared with the average, ESP teachers require longer experience, higher qualifications, and the morale that relishes each fresh set of learners as a professional challenge. Consequently:

(ii) *ESP teachers are more expensive,* being generally somewhat older, better-qualified, and in short supply.

(iii) *ESP requires considerable preparation time.* Although frequent practice brings improvements, every fresh ESP learner or group of learners requires an analysis of precise needs; the design of a suitable syllabus; collaboration with a relevant subject specialist; the writing of suitable materials, including tests where appropriate; the preparation of the teachers. As a rough guide, a new ESP course of, say, 10 weeks' duration, will require between 3 and 5 weeks of preparation by roughly the same number of people who will be teaching on the course. Consequently:

(iv) *The direct costs of ESP per student week are markedly higher* for the two reasons adduced above: (a) more expensive teachers; (b) additional prior preparation time.

Trying to avoid these prerequisites is unwise and futile. The result is likely to be either that the teaching is not truly ESP but only labelled so; or that the success which *can* be achieved will not be. It cannot be too strongly stressed—and it is the professional duty of ESP teachers to ensure that this is made clear to their administrative masters—firstly, that the very real benefits of ESP can only be achieved by employing teachers capable of working at the required higher professional level; secondly, that extra preparation time *must* be allowed for; and, thirdly, that in consequence ESP is both more sophisticated than 'general English' *and more expensive.*

ESP and methodology

It is, of course, apparent that ESP is not itself a methodology. But neither is it allied to or associated with any particular teaching techniques. Indeed, the matching of the teaching to the learner's needs also extends freedom to innovate in methodological terms also. This is perhaps one of the major attractions which ESP offers to the experienced teacher: instead of being constrained within methods consecrated by years of repetition, the teacher of ESP is very frequently able to make a real choice, on professional grounds, between the many possibilities that form part of the training and experience of the mature teacher. If there is any single problem in the area of methodology that is greater for the ESP teacher than for the teacher of 'general English' it is that ESP learners who are already specialists in a particular subject or occupation tend to have strong expectations that they will *and should* be taught English along the same methodological lines as they may have experienced at school, 10 or 20 years before. Again, part of the challenge of ESP lies in finding acceptable ways of overcoming prejudices of this kind and persuading the mature student that it is nowadays possible to help him to learn better, faster, and more enjoyably, within the confines of ESP, than his early experience might lead him to expect. The competent ESP teacher knows that learning can be successful, and he or she can enjoy bringing the realization of this success to the ESP learner.

Bibliographical note

Comprehensive bibliographies of ESP and the wider issues touched on in this paper can be found in:

British Council (1979) *Information Guide No. 2: English for Specific Purposes,* London.

Cowan J. Ronayne (ed.) (1977) *Special Issue on Language for Special Purposes: Studies in Language Learning,* Vol. 2, No. 1, Fall, 1977, Urbana-Champaign, Illinois.

Robinson, P. (1980) *English for Specific Purposes (ESP),* Pergamon Press, Oxford.

Strevens, Peter (1978) Special-purpose language learning: a perspective' in G Perren (ed.), *Linguistics and Language Learning: Surveys,* CILT, London.

Chapter 10

Technical, Technological, and Scientific English (TTSE)

The greatest effort in teaching English to speakers of other languages has been concentrated on English as a general educational and cultural subject, taught within the framework of a school system. This kind of English teaching is still of very great importance. As we have seen in Chapter 9, there now exists, in addition to conventional English teaching, a large and growing demand for English language teaching to be provided specifically for the needs of a particular subject, profession, or occupation; and for this teaching to be carried on largely outside the school system. Within the wide range of vocational uses of English we can identify a group concerned with pure or applied science at various levels of complexity. In this chapter we shall consider the nature of the English used for such purposes, and we shall touch on some of the problems that arise in teaching it.

The labels 'scientific English' or 'technical English' are often used, though without being closely defined or distinguished from one another. In fact, it is not so much the features of the English that determine the choice of label as the purposes for which the English is used. My own preference is for a three-part distinction, between *science, technology,* and *technical services;* each of these has a separate function and can be shown to employ language in a different way. At the same time there are a number of features common to all three subdivisions. Before looking at each of these separately we should consider what they have in common.

Features in common and separate

TTSE makes use of the same phonology, the same orthography, and the same grammar as do other uses of English. There is no special accent for talking about science; the spelling is the same; the same pronouns, tenses, word-order, etc., are used, and so on. As to grammar, TTSE employs Standard English and it occurs in both spoken and written forms. The vocabulary of TTSE is partly common-core and partly special to itself. In addition to these common features, TTSE alone employs an elaborate range of written symbols, chiefly but not solely those of mathematics, which link in with the extensive use of numbers.

Beyond the obvious features of grammar, phonology, graphology, and lexis, TTSE is used in order to express a large number of concepts and to conduct a number of intellectual processes. Some of the concepts and processes are shared with English in general, while others are confined to science or even to particular branches of science. Finally, the contexts in which TTSE is used are almost always specific to science, technology, or technical work.

Grammatical and rhetorical features of TTSE

In pointing out that TTSE makes use of the same grammar as do other uses of English one is merely affirming that 'scientific English is a variety of English'. But in fact the recurrent grammatical patterns of TTSE are characteristic and are different from those of other varieties.

Although he is not as a rule consciously aware of them, the educated native speaker of English is very sensitive to grammatical features such as: sentence length (i.e. the number of clauses contained in sentences); type and sequence of clauses within a sentence, relative frequency of main and subordinate clauses; order of the subject in relation to the main verb, and the amount of variation in this sequence; number of adjuncts (adverbial and prepositional phrases) and their location initially or finally in the clause; relative frequency of particular verb-forms (e.g. passive or active, tense, aspect, etc.); reference forward or backward in the text; and several others. One specialist (R. V. White) has successfully used in undergraduate teaching a specification of these and other grammatical features in a text, but without specifying the lexis of the text, to elicit an identification of the kind of text is must have been. TTSE texts are fairly easily identifiable in terms of these and other grammatical patterns.

It has often been observed that scientific texts employ verbs in their passive forms to a greater extent than most non-scientific texts. But is has also often been stated, I believe wrongly, that this happens because science is 'impersonal' and therefore it is necessary to use *it* as a subject instead of *I, you, he, she, we,* or *they,* or *Dr. X.* An alternative explanation for using the passive is concerned not with a choice between 'personal' or 'impersonal' expression but with the nature of the *rhetoric* of English sentences and of much scientific writing. The organization of clauses in English is such that *initial* position for the subject (as in passive constructions) is normally the strongest.

Compare these sentences:

(i) *The temperature of the solution is maintained at 60°C by a thermostat.*

(ii) *A thermostat maintains the temperature of the solution at 60°C.*

In terms of rhetoric, sentence (i) is 'about' the temperature of the solution; sentence (ii) is 'about' a thermostat. The choice of passive voice for the verb is dictated by the theme of the text at that point, not by notions about personal or impersonal constructions.

Concepts expressed in TTSE

Certain conceptual relationships are common to all advanced and complex thought, no matter what the subject, and these general concepts are expressed in English by the use of items such as *although, because, if, unless, until, whenever,* etc. The scientist who cannot handle items of this kind, together with grammatical features such as subordination, relativization, co-ordination, etc., in English cannot handle science in English; but he cannot handle any other discipline, either.

The importance of these general concepts in advanced thought is that they state the logic—the rhetoric, the argument—of the text, as well as having grammatical consequences. They do not fit into any single grammatical category, and it may be convenient here to call them logico-grammatical items. These can be grouped into a number of classes according to the notions they convey. There are approximately 100 items, in about seven notional classes (see Appendix A); the following examples give only three items in each class, to serve as illustrations:

Linking and logical sequence of ideas
   furthermore, thus, in addition to . . .
Paraphrase and apposition
   like, similarly, as if . . .
Causality
   because, therefore, as a result of . . .
Opposition or contrast
   however, nevertheless, in spite of . . .
Restriction
   except, unless, only if . . .
Hypothesis
   conclude, refute, suppose . . .
Enquiry
   how big, long, many? . . . with what purpose? to what extent?

A second type comprises those concepts which are general to science and technology but not typically present in non-scientific English. These concepts reflect and convey the philosophy and methodology of science. At this point we touch on a central dilemma in the teaching of English for use by scientists, technologists, and technicians. The phrase 'philosophy and methodology of science' conveys to those who have been trained in them a considerable set of beliefs, attitudes, assumptions, values, and ethics. To the non-scientist, the extent and nature of these ideas are wholly or partly hidden. And yet when the scientist learns English it is almost always a non-scientist who has the task of teaching it to him. In a brief paper it is impossible to resolve the dilemma. One can only point to its existence and assure the arts-trained teacher that being a scientist or technologist entails learning a number of habits of thought, that these habits of thought directly affect his use of language, and that the scientist can only function as a scientist if he learns how to use language appropriately to these habits of thought.

As a rough approximation, one can summarize the scientist's mental operations thus: the philosophy of science entails concepts of *discrimination and description, classification, interrelation,* and *explanation,* often in that order. (See Appendix B.) And each of these concepts in turn implies other concepts, which make up the methodology of science:

> *Discrimination and description* imply concepts of *identity and difference processes, states, changes of state, quantification*
>
> *Classification* implies concepts of *taxonomies* and the *co-occurrence of features*
>
> *Interrelation* implies concepts of *causality, influence,* and *interaction*
>
> *Explanation* implies concepts of *evidence, intuition, hypothesis, experiment, models, theory,* etc.

Quantification

One of these concepts that causes particular difficulties to non-scientist teachers of English is *quantification*. It is worth noting that scientists need to be able not only to *write* quantities in mathematical symbols (which forms part of their basic scientific training) but also to *understand* numbers, algebraic symbols, equations, formulae, etc., when spoken in English, and perhaps even to *speak* them. There are linguistic problems in verbalizing in English an expression like:

$$n(x,y,z) = \sqrt{\left[1 - \frac{F(x,y,z)}{hv}\right]^2 - \frac{v_o{}^2}{v^2}}$$

Nevertheless, the rules for verbalizing quantities and expressions are conventional and can be taught—once the teacher knows them.

All scientific texts, then, will typically make use, as may be appropriate, of the logico-grammatical items and of concepts general to science. In addition, depending on the particular branch of science concerned, particular subsets of concepts may be employed. For example, in a work on *zoology,* a writer may refer to concepts of *respiration, reproduction, water-relations,* etc.; while in a lecture on *acoustics* a speaker may refer to concepts of *frequency, spectrum, bandwidth, phase,* etc. These more specific concepts in turn require the use of specialized terms. This is where a consideration of TTSE must turn to questions of vocabulary.

TTSE vocabulary and terminology
The vocabulary of TTSE contains words and expressions of three main kinds: (i) the vocabulary of scientific concepts as already outlined; (ii) overlapping with this, a stock of words composed of Greek and Latin roots and affixes having international acceptance and currency; and (iii) a number of other special scientific and technological coinings.

During the past 200 years, scientists working in the Western European tradition have abandoned the former use of Latin as the only appropriate language for scientific discourse. But in accepting other languages—English, French, German, Spanish, Portuguese, Russian, etc.—as being suitable vehicles for writing and talking about science, they have, nonetheless, maintained in use a sublanguage of roots, prefixes, and suffixes, either borrowed from Classical or Medieval Latin or Greek, or newly coined with Greek or Latin elements. Every scientist needs to be familiar with about fifty prefixes (e.g. *a-, anti-, auto-, contra- ex-, intra-, mono-, pre-, syn-, trans-, un-,* etc.), about thirty suffixes (e.g. *-able, -al, -ic, -ise, -meter, -phage,* etc.), and about 100 roots (e.g. *bio, calor, geo, tele, dermis, therm,* etc.). (See Appendix C.)

Scientific and technical terms not using Greek or Latin elements are numerous and new ones are continuously being coined, e.g. *peening, milling, count-down, hardware, de-bugging, bit, byte,* etc. The learning of a special vocabulary seems to be less of a problem to the learner than it may appear to the English-language teacher. The scientist has acquired a conceptual framework into which new terminology fits relatively easily compared with the puzzlement of the arts-trained teacher when faced with such terms.

Jargon

When discussing specialist vocabulary, the word *jargon* is sometimes used. But increasingly it seems to convey the meaning 'I don't understand your technical terms and I dislike it when you use them'. Scientists themselves rarely use the word *jargon* except as a form of apology for using technical terms in the presence of non-scientists, while non-scientists tend to use the word in situations where they feel excluded from understanding what is being said simply because technical terms have been used. The word *jargon* is thus concerned with the good manners of communication between scientists and non-scientists; it is also used in referring to 'badly written' science. It is not a synonym for 'scientific vocabulary'.

Scientific, technological, technical

It is now possible to explain and justify the distinction made in this paper between three kinds of language use. Each refers to a major branch of scientific activity which uses English in a distinctive way. First, we can state the different task of each subdivision:

Science is concerned with understanding, describing, and explaining the nature of the universe (including, of course, Man).

Technology is concerned with how to design, operate, and control machines, devices and instruments.

Technical services are concerned with how to construct and maintain the devices invented by technology according to the principles established in science.

Not surprisingly, these different tasks lead to different uses of English, which can be described according to the different mixture of features which each displays.

'Scientific English' uses the full range of general and scientific concepts, philosophical as well as methodological; it uses the stock of international scientific terminology based on Greek and Latin roots, the terms of particular branches of science, and other coinings; it assumes familiarity with the symbols and visual conventions of mathematics, but except in the field of mathematics itself it uses less numerical quantification than occurs in technology.

'*Technological English*' makes less use than does 'Scientific English' of general conceptual language, but it makes full use of special vocabulary and is strong in its use of numerical quantification and mathematical symbols; there is more reference to the concrete and the practical, as contrasted with more use of the abstract and the philosophical in 'Scientific English'.

'*Technical English*' uses little of the language of general, philosophical, or even methodological concepts; the special terminology used relates chiefly to concrete objects and practical processes rather than to abstractions; quantification is mainly a matter of stating measurements rather than the symbolization of mathematical relationships; there is a good deal of non-scientific or 'common-core' English interspersed in technical texts.

What has been said in the paper about TTSE is far from being an exhaustive description of it. Indeed, by its very nature it is barely conceivable that a complete description of TTSE could ever be made, since it consists of the expression in English of the purposes of the scientist. But the outline may serve to introduce the teacher of English to the nature of the language he is required to teach.

Teaching TTSE

Few teachers of English have a scientific training. The conventional pattern of English teaching in the past has been as a general educational and cultural subject, taught in schools, and for this purpose the training of teachers in the traditions of the humanities has seemed to be appropriate. It is a consequence of this tradition, however, that teachers of English called upon to teach English for the uses of scientists face special problems. They have to learn something of the habits of thought of the scientist and they have to become aware of the nature of TTSE. Beyond this, they may even have to construct their own teaching materials, since very few suitable textbooks or courses yet exist.

Two main alternatives offer themselves as an approach to the teaching of TTSE. The first is to teach TTSE as a *special-purpose* course after the learner has already learned 'common-core' English in a conventional course. The second is to produce an *integrated* course in which the science or technology syllabus is taught with and through the language syllabus.

Under certain circumstances, special-purpose TTSE courses, topping-up a basis of common-core English, can be very effective, Such courses can be highly specific; they can often be taught intensively over a short period; since the learners are usually adults with good motivation, they tend to co-operate with the teacher, to work enthusiastically and to achieve a high rate of success. But there are dangers, too. In some countries the fact of having followed a long course in English at school (perhaps for 10 or 12 years) is no guarantee that a practical grasp of the common core of English has in fact been acquired, so that a special-purpose course in TTSE has to be preceded by an emergency course in English from scratch. Before special-purpose courses are decided upon, a realistic assessment of the average level of achievement in English must first be made.

One particular type of special-purpose course must be mentioned: it is sometimes the case that scientists of technologists need to acquire a reading-only knowledge of English (or another foreign language) in their own branch of science, with no requirement to understand the spoken language or to speak. Such restricted aims permit the course-designer to dispense with large components of conventional language-teaching courses (particularly the whole of teaching the spoken language) and therefore to reach the target more quickly. A restricted aim can also be more accurately defined than can the aims of full-scale language teaching. Since the scientist is normally an intelligent, sophisticated learner, who is virtually always a volunteer and not a conscript, the circumstances of teaching reading-only courses for scientists are very favourable indeed: progress is usually rapid and success rates are high.

The integrated course, in which English is taught by and through science, seems in principle to be the most economical and satisfactory approach, not least because the teacher can devote the whole of the teaching time to activities that are relevant to the eventual aims of the learner. This is in contrast to the most frequently adopted approach, where the future scientist spends a great deal of time on arts-oriented language work in his basic course before he starts his final special-purpose TTSE course.

If integrated courses are theoretically more efficient in learning and teaching time, they are also extremely difficult to design. The conventional course, with its orientation towards general educational, cultural, and usually literary activities, has a long history. Fifty years of intense professional activity has led to the emergence of a range of syllabuses, drills and exercises, aural and visual aids, and tests and examinations. Although there are far from ideal, at least they exist; they provide the course-writer with a vast mine of experience out of which he can develop new materials for particular purposes. But the integrated course for TTSE has a much shorter history, so that those who are currently engaged in producing such courses are dependent on their own resources. What is more, the integrated course requires that not only the English teaching but also the science teaching should be impeccable, and this usually requires close collaboration between writers from the two different specialities.

The English-teaching profession needs in the coming years a large number of publications dealing with all aspects of TTSE, and the sharing of experience in trying various techniques and approaches. There is no doubt that the demand for TTSE is going to increase. It offers a challenge to the teaching profession, but one which most teachers will find it exciting to meet.

Appendix A. Some classes of logico-grammatical items
NB: These categories are 'notional'; they are not presented in order of importance; the categories and lists are not exhaustive.

Linking and logical sequence of ideas: and, also, besides, furthermore, moreover, simultaneously, thus, too; apart from, as well as, in addition to.

Paraphrase and apposition: like, similarly; as if, in the same way, in like manner.

Causality: accordingly, as, because, consequently, hence, once (something has occurred), since, therefore, until, whenever; as long as, as a result of, by means of, due to, for the purpose of, in order to, it follows that, on account of, owing to; necessary and sufficient condition.

Opposition or contrast: alternatively, although, but, if, however, nevertheless, notwithstanding, otherwise, whereas, yet; even though, in spite of, irrespective of, on the other hand; necessary but not sufficient condition.

Restriction: except, impossible, occasionally, only, trivial, uncertain, unless; if, if and only if, only when.

Hypothesis: conclude, confirm, consider, deduce, imagine, infer, invalidate, refute, suppose, theoretically, validate; in principle, it follows, it would seem that . . .

Enquiry: how big? how long? how many? . . . etc; what? when? which? who? why? how? with what purpose? to what end? to what extent?

Appendix B: Concepts in the philosophy and methodology of Science

Philosophical concepts	*Methodological concepts*
	Identity and difference
Descrimination and description	Characteristics, qualities, features
	Processes
	States and changes of state
	Quantification
	Taxonomies
Classification	Co-occurrence of features
	Distribution
	Comprehensiveness
	Causality
Interrelationship	Influence
	Interaction
	Evidence
	Intuition
	Hypothesis
Explanation	Experiment
	Models
	Theory

Appendix C: Some prefixes, roots, and suffixes of Greek and Latin origins, with examples and approximate 'meanings'

1. *Prefixes:*

a-	atypical	a = not
ab-	abnormal	ab = away from
ad-	adhesion	ad = to, towards
anti-	**antiseptic**	anti = against
ante-	ante-natal	ante = before (in time)
auto-	automotive	auto = from within itself
bi-	biennial	bi = two
co-	cohesion	co = with

N.B. *co-* has others forms: *con-* as in *connect*; *com-* as in *communicate*; *cor-* as in *correlate*; *col-* as in *collaborate*.

contra-	contra-rotation	contra = opposite
de-	defuse	de = take away, undo
dia-	diathermy	dia = through
dis-	dismember	dis = undo, un-make
dys	dystrophy	dys = out of order, functioning badly
ex-	extract	ex = away from, out of (or formerly)
extra-	extra-sensory	extra = outside
in-	(a) inject, inflame, etc.	in = (a) into
	(b) inoffensive, incapable	in = (b) not

N.B. *in-* has other forms: *il-* as in *illogical*; *im-* as in *immovable*; *ir-* as in *irregular*.

inter-	international	inter = from one to another
intra-	intra-uterine	intra = within
macro-	macro-economics	macro = relatively large
micro-	microwave	micro = relatively small
mono-	monotonous	mono = single
non-	non-toxic	non = not
poly-	polyvalent	poly = many
post-	postpone	post = later
pre-	prehistoric	pre = before

re-	re-cycle	re = again
sub-	sub-zero	sub = below
super-	superficial	super = upon, above
syn-	synthesis	syn = together

N.B. *syn-* has other forms: *syl-* as in *syllogism*; *sym-* as in *symmetrical*.

trans-	transmission	trans = across, from place to place
un-	unstable	un = not
uni-	unitary	uni = single

2. *Roots:*
(a) Examples where the root is word-initial

bio-	biology, biotic	bio = life
calor-	calorific	calor = heat
chrono-	chronological	chrono = time
cycl-	cyclic	cycl = repeating
geo-	geophysical	geo = the Earth
magni-	magnifying	magni = large in size
meteor-	meteorology	meteor = the atmosphere
tele-	telemetry	tele = at a distance
zoo-	zoology	zoo = life

(b) Examples where the root is non-initial

-derm	epidermis	derm = skin
-gon	polygonal	gon = angle, corner
-ion	thermionic	ion = electrical particle
-lumen,		
-lumin	illuminate	lumen = light
-mini	diminish	mini = small
-therm	diathermy	therm = heat
-tox	intoxicate	tox = poison

3. *Suffixes:*

-able	intractable	-able = cable of having some-
-ible	inexhaustible	-ible = thing done
-al	oral	-al = an adjective
-ate	vibrate	-ate = to carry out a process or action

-ation	vibration	-ation = the process of doing something
-ator	vibrator	-ator = the object or person carrying out a process or action
-ic	electric	-ic = having a particular quality
-ise (or US -ize)	computerise	-ise = to apply a process or bring about a particular change
-logy	psephology	-logy = the study of a particular field of knowledge
-meter	calorimeter	-meter = measuring device

Chapter 11

Problems of Learning and Teaching Science through a Foreign Language

Most studies in the philosophy and the practice of science education embody two unstated assumptions: first, that the learner is a member of the same culture and is accustomed to the same general educational system, values, and procedures, as those within which the studies of science education were prepared; and, second, that the teacher and the learner have as their common mother tongue the language in which the science is being taught.

For very many millions of learners and teachers these assumptions are false, and their falsity accounts in large part for shortcomings in the learning and teaching of science, chiefly in the 'developing countries' but also among some minority groups in the 'technologically developed countries' e.g. immigrants, native speakers of languages such as Gaelic, Breton, Eskimo, etc., in which science education is usually not provided.

This chapter surveys the kinds of language problems encountered by science educators and learners of science when the vehicle of instruction is not their mother tongue, and describes a convergence of interests between two different groups of educators: (a) those who teach science through the medium of a foreign language, and (b) those who teach a foreign language to learners whose principal aims include the learning of science.

In practice, the great majority of cases involve the teaching of science in and through *English,* and the convergence referred to is a convergence by teachers of *English* for science and technology. The principles are identical when the language of instruction is French, or Spanish, or Russian, or any other international language not the mother tongue of the science learner. But the examples and the elaboration of principles have arisen chiefly in the context of English as a foreign language, which will therefore be used in this chapter as a paradigm example for the general case of science education in a foreign language.

I

The size of the problem is immense, though precise statistics are not available. A major branch of science education has been engaged for three decades in meeting the growing demand from developing countries for the expansion of mathematics and science teaching, in a context of a great expansion of education in general but within severe limitations of money, facilities, and teacher-training programmes. Part of the response to this demand has taken the form of 'drives' on science education by the provision of large numbers of expatriate English-speaking science teachers through special schemes of governmental aid, and by the organization from Britain and the United States of large-scale curriculum-reform and teacher-training projects directed specifically towards the developing countries. Hundreds of thousands of teachers, perhaps millions, indigenous to these countries are now teaching science according to syllabuses and using teaching methods that originated in Britain or the United States, and their teaching is mostly carried out in English, a language foreign equally to them and to their pupils. These circumstances raise questions about the consequences of using a foreign language in teaching and learning science, and also about the effectiveness with which English has been taught to teachers of science as part of their general education and their professional training.

At the level of anecdote and day-to-day experience, the types of language difficulty encountered by science teachers from Britain and the United States working overseas are fairly well known. They include problems such as the following:

(i) general, unanalysed difficulties of mutual comprehension between teacher and pupil, especially in spoken English;

(ii) the absence, in the learner's own language, of a word or expression equivalent to one in English, e.g. *electricity, octagonal, expansion;*

(iii) the absence, in the learner's own language or culture, of a necessary concept, e.g. *infinity, zero, gravity* (this is a more difficult problem than the absence of a word for an object or process which can be illustrated or displayed, and it entails difficult explanations of an intellectual kind);

(iv) word-order difficulties of two or more kinds: (a) in English statements, the typical word order is subject-verb-object, but many languages have other orders into which learners may unthinkingly transpose their English when referring to science: e.g. Amharic speakers may verbalize $4+2=6$ as 'four and two six is' (R. W. Morris in UNESCO-CEDO-1CM1, 1974); (b) in English, adjectives typically precede nouns, in a given ordered sequence, but in many other languages they may follow the noun and take a different sequence, e.g. Eng. *The dominant statistical index*: French *l'indice statistique dominant*: transferred into English (e.g. as *the index statistical dominant*) this can cause confusion and incomprehension;

(v) lack of familiarity on the part of the learner with even the common, everday roots from Greek or Latin which enter into scientific vocabulary, e.g. *geo-, therm-, zoo-, kilo-, multi-, ante-, anti-,* etc.

(vi) lack of precision in the use of language, e.g. using indifferently *if, when, whenever, as a result of,* etc.

(vii) interference from non-decimal counting systems.

But it is easier to understand the nature of the difficulties if they are analysed under a number of more generalized headings:

I. Language differences between teacher and learner

There is a wide range of possible communication problems between teacher and learner when science is taught in English to learners for whom it is a foreign language. If the teacher is a native speaker of English (e.g. if he is an 'expatriate' science teacher) his fluency, rapidity, use of metaphors and idioms and unfamiliar accent all constitute impediments to the learner's understanding of the science lesson, even when the learner has a good command of English. But such impediments are normally transient: once one understands one variety of a foreign language it is relatively simple to learn to understand another variety. Teachers, too, learn to accommodate their speech to the more obvious difficulties of their pupils.

To re-state the matter, the command of English for science purposes by the teacher and by the pupil may be either adequate or less than adequate. In some cases, both learner and teacher may have inadequate English, in which case science learning is unlikely. More often, the teacher's command is adequate, the learner's command is inadequate but gradually improves. On occasion, especially in the teaching of more advanced science, it transpires that the teacher's command of English is adequate for everyday use and for elementary mathematics or science but is inadequate for higher-level teaching. Or the teacher may be entirely capable in English when *reading* or *writing,* but is unable *to speak* satisfactorily in the English of science.

None of these cases is irremediable, and techniques exist, within English-teaching methodology, for helping either the learner or the teacher towards the necessary improvement.

In many parts of the world, learners of science may know little English but be fluent in pidgin, and this can cause special problems of comprehension in the field of science. A pidgin is a lingua franca having enormous geographical coverage. Pidgins are nobody's mother tongue, by definition; all the many millions of speakers of pidgins have picked them up as a foreign language. Until recently pidgins have been regarded as simplified versions of English with an admixture of other languages. It is now proposed that pidgins may stand closer to a basic form of human language and that English could be regarded as a 'complexification' from such a primal form.

At all events, although teachers of science will welcome the ability of pidgin speakers to understand some parts of English, they will be put out to find that other parts—plural distinctions, complex tenses, conditionals, etc.—are absent from their pupils' comprehension of English. Pidgin could not be used for the communicative purposes of science without a great deal of further development.

II. Degree of adaptation for science in the learner's language

There is overwhelming evidence that *any* language is potentially able to be developed so as to express all the communication needs of the people who speak it, including scientific discourse of all kinds. But this is a statement of potentiality, not actuality. Very many languages have not yet developed terms, words, expressions, modes of meaning, for communicating about science. When a learner of science is a native speaker of a language not yet adapted to the purposes of science, his learning through English entails very special, additional difficulties of cognition and understanding. He cannot appeal to translation into his mother tongue for the resolution of doubt or the dissipation of ignorance; if he encounters, for example, the word *hypothesis* in his science textbook, there is likely to be no exactly equivalent item in his own language. He is denied the support of the surprisingly international—in terms of European languages—vocabulary of scientific terms constructed from Greek or Latin roots.

There are several examples in recent times (Israel, Malaysia, Tanzania, etc.) of countries deliberately setting out to hasten the development of a scientific register for their own languages, and to incorporate the learning and teaching of the new terms *and new concepts* in the educational system. It is necessary to emphasize the fact that concepts are involved, as well as words, since what is occurring is that a set of concepts, relationships, operations, until now unfamiliar in the language and culture, are being deliberately incorporated therein. To add a term presupposes adding the concept; to provide a 'name' alone does not necessarily establish understanding of a concept.

III. Extent and kind of science in the learner's culture

This discussion touched first on the *language* of science because it is the creation of terminology which most obviously presents a problem. But underlying the linguistic facts are the *social and cultural realities.* A language without equivalents for particular scientific terms is a language spoken by people who do not (yet) possess a sizeable group of science users. But it is an error to suppose that such a society engages in no scientific activity. Take the basic scientific feature of measurement: a language and its culture may have no equivalents of *metre, yard, area, hour, north.,* etc. But it is certain to possess some forms of measurement. Thus Taiwo describes systems of measurement of the Yoruba, a society in Western Nigeria:

'Measures are seldom exact, since they depend upon practical situations, and employ approximation in accordance with the magnitude of that which is susceptible to measurement. Thus the unit for short distances is "ese", the foot length. For cloth measure it is the "awe", being a full arm span from the tips of the middle fingers when both arms are outstretched. For long distances, the measure is the "ibuso", about a mile, or the distance a man carrying an average head load would go before making a short stop to stretch his neck. Areas of farms are measured by the number of yam heaps that could be planted—about six heaps to ten square yards. . . .

'Weight and measures of weight are new ideas. The Yoruba compare weights by lifting the articles in turn and declaring which is heavier. As a result of the lack of measures of weights, commodities which are sold by weight in other communities are sold in Yorubaland by the set or in piles.

'Although cowries as legal tender are dead and buried . . . they are used in expressing big numbers simply. For example, the use of the unit "oke" (20,000) makes big numbers more easily comprehensible. In their pound, shilling and pence equivalents, they are used in expressing areas of farmland and the number of crops . . . "nine pence" of land is an acre and "nine pence" of cocoa trees is 3,000 cocoa trees.' (Taiwo, in UNESCO-CEDO-ICMI, 1974.)

The essential point here is that although a society and language may not employ concepts and terms that are identical with those of Western science, they will certainly have some concepts and terms which refer to number, measurement, agriculture, architecture, engineering, medicine, botany, and other fields of scientific activity. The cognitive task for the learner of science through English, then, is not the finding of translation equivalents in his own language for scientific terminology, nor yet to write science upon a *tabula rasa,* but the acquisition of fresh attitudes towards observation and of terms for ideas which are partly new to him and partly just different from those already familiar to him.

In these circumstances, the science educator must watch for the unwitting presence in his teaching of ideas which are baffling to the learner though self-evident to the European or American teacher. For example, a young learner from a society which measures time by sunrise and sunset, and whose family does not possess a watch or clock, will at first regard as mysterious any classroom exercises which involve the precise measurement of time. To give another example from actual experience in Zambia (pre-independence), textbook illustrations comparing a very tall, muscular young man with a tiny, wizened old man with a beard, intended to contrast the concepts GREATER and LESSER respectively, may be interpreted according to the local cultural tradition that 'any older man is to be valued more highly than any younger man', implying the contrast LESSER versus GREATER and so reversing the pedagogical (and mathematical) intention of the example.

IV. Degree of familiarity with science and its reasoning-system
The learner may have been brought up in a culture in which magic and the supernatural play a great part: consequently the child may be accustomed (a) to accepting relationships, reasons, justifications, etc., being of a non-logical kind ('The rain comes because we make our sacrifices in the proper way'); (b) to believing statements simply because they are made by people in customary authority ('My English teacher says science is ruining the world'); (c) to equating the technically complex with the supernatural ('He must be a wizard: he can mix medicines to cure any illness'). From the standpoint of science education, such beliefs and attitudes and schemes of reasoning create barriers to learning. They can probably be changed, or accommodated to, but first they have to be recognized and identified, and then the approach to them by the science teacher has to be made with great caution and sympathy so as not to trigger resentment in the learner or his community. In the complex processes of cultural adaptation on the

part of pre-industrial societies to the encroachment of ideas from industrial societies, the simple statement of scientific principles may look like a new kind of colonialism and be justifiably resented if it is not made in the knowledge and acceptance of cultural differences.

The relevance of these observations on cultural contact lies in the fact that many of the learner's difficulties with the foreign language, English, reflect not just linguistic problems but problems of his adjustment to a culture and a language which requires the expression of some subtly different presuppositions and attitudes towards, for example, causality, precision, quantification, etc.

V. Relative stages of education development

Reference has already been made to the mounting of 'drives' in science education in which the most recent educational developments and the most up-to-date curricula are embodied in a major project of materials preparation, teacher training, and educational improvement. Such drives (which are also familiar in other subject areas) encounter a range of difficulties analysed by Beeby (1966) in terms of stages of national educational development. Beeby postulates a developmental sequence through four stages: (1) *'Dame school' stage:*'. . . the bulk of the teachers are ill-educated and . . . have had only the sketchiest training.' In this stage the teaching is '. . . *confusedly and inefficiently* formal' (Beeby's italics). The syllabus is vague and narrow. (2) *Stage of formalism*: the teachers are ill-educated, but trained. Learning is classroom-bound. Teaching methods are rigid. (3) *Stage of transition*: the teachers are trained and better educated, and are becoming prepared for stage (4) *Stage of Meaning*: the teachers are well-educated and trained, and they encourage pupils to think for themselves. There is an '. . . attempt to give each child a deeper and wider understanding of the symbols with which he works.' 'The subjects of the curriculum may not be very different from those at stage (3), but their content will be wider and more varied.' 'Meaning and understanding play an increasing part in the pupils' day, and memorizing and drill, while still remaining, become subservient to them' (Beeby, op. cit.).

Most science education drives in developing countries in recent years have been devised as exponents of stage (4) education; although their primary purpose has been the improvement of science education, they have always contained a secondary aim, that of disseminating the highest current standards of education in general—as these standards are understood in countries which have reached Beeby's stage (4).

Two consequences arise. The first is that it turns out to be exceptionally difficult to transplant stage (4) educational techniques into countries where (say) stage (2) is the norm, and to require considerable periods of time, especially in retraining the teachers and improving their own personal level of education—which in the context of the present argument means improving their command of the English needed for teaching science.

The second consequence is linked to the first. The kinds of teaching technique that are required in modern, stage (4) science projects, concentrating as they do on the learner's understanding, on discovery procedures, and on guidance to learn rather than on memorization, all require *more talk* on the part of the teacher. For the expatriate teacher this is not a problem, rather the reverse. But the local teacher who is teaching science in a foreign language, English, often finds that the new techniques make demands upon his command of spoken English which he is unable to meet. Very frequently the teacher's English is insufficient to enable him to teach in the ways encouraged by the new science programmes.

This is not a criticism of such projects nor of the value of science education drives in themselves. It is simply a reminder that a drive on one subject or group of subjects may have unexpected links with other subject areas: in this case, with the teaching of English to those who will become teachers of science, a topic to which we shall return.

II

The foregoing discussion has loosely grouped the kinds of language problems encountered in science education overseas according to five *ad hoc* headings. A more principled framework can be proposed for identifying and explaining possible sources of language difficulty in science education. It is adapted from an unpublished working paper by M. A. K. Halliday. (See also Halliday in UNESCO-CEDO-ICMI, 1974.)

Sources of difficulty may be *linguistic* (i.e. originating in the properties of language 'as a system') or *sociolinguistic* (i.e. originating in the nature of language 'as a social institution').

1. *Linguistic difficulties*: these may be of three kinds:

(a) *Meanings*—'semantic difficulties'. The learner must learn the appropriate meanings of science and how they are expressed in English. They are of two main types:

    (i) arguments—the 'rhetoric' of scientific communication;
    (ii) single items—e.g. terminology, logical operators, etc.

(b) *Words and structures*—'lexico-grammar'. In order to understand and express the meanings of science the learner must acquire command of the three kinds of language rules for doing so:

    (i) sentence and phrase structures—'syntax', the rules for constructing and comprehending sentences;
    (ii) words—'vocabulary', the items (with meanings) which string together in phrases and sentences;
    (iii) word structures—'morphology', the rules for constructing words in English, which includes the large stock of words borrowed from Greek and Latin, e.g. knowing that *physics* is not *physic* plus plural *-s* but *phys-* plus *-ics,* and hence is a singular noun whose meaning describes an area of intellectual inquiry.

(c) *Symbols*—the learner must be aware of the degree and kind of correspondence, and be able to handle the rules for conversion between writing and speech, of chemical formulae, mathematical notation, and other scientific symbolizations.

2. *Sociolinguistic difficulties*: these will be principally determined by two kinds of variables:

(a) *The functional status of English* when used as the medium of science education:

  (i) *in general*—how widely is English used in the society in question?

  (ii) *special*—how familiar in the local society is the English of science?

(b) *'Distance' of English from the learner's mother tongue:*

  (i) *in status*—the learner's expectations and achievements are much affected by whether English, as a language, is valued low or highly in his community;

  (ii) *in world view and meaning styles*—particularly whether Western science, logic and reasoning systems are familiar;

  (iii) *in internal structure*—the more closely English approximates to the learner's mother tongue in syntax, vocabulary, word-structure, sound-systems, and writing systems, the smaller will be the language barrier in general and the smaller will be the impediment to his learning of science through English.

III

It is now appropriate to consider the ways in which the language educators, in particular the teachers of English as a foreign language, have recently become engaged in an aspect of science education, thus forming the convergence referred to earlier.

As we have noted at many points in this book, until about 1960 it was tacitly assumed throughout the world that the teaching of English overseas formed part of a general education, that it belonged specifically among the humanities and certainly not among the science subjects, and that the very best pupils would go on to study English literature at university level. If a pupil's command of English was used by him to learn science, this way a by-product of no interest to the teacher of English.

As more and more countries gained political independence from Britain and France, and as school education became more widely available in developing countries, there arose a demand for English-language teaching to be offered independently of literature, with its presumptions of moral and cultural value systems. The attitude widely expressed was: 'We need the English language as a tool for international communication, but we have no wish to teach our children the moral values of Englishmen and Americans.' English thus began to be taught increasingly, though not universally, for the purpose of giving the learner a good practical command of the language, including the spoken language, for whatever purposes he might ultimately have.

Since 1970 a further development has occurred and has grown with startling rapidity. Many learners, especially adults, found that they needed to be able to use English for specific purposes, either in their occupation or for study. At the same time, language educators began to develop techniques for teaching limited-objective courses, often at high rates of intensity and with considerable success. There thus emerged *English for Special Purposes* (ESP), of which *English for Science and Technology* (EST) is the most important branch.

ESP has grown very fast, in higher and further education, i.e. for adult learners either in colleges and universities or already in employment. Its relatively high rates of success and of 'customer satisfaction', together with the attractive rationale of teaching a language for specific aims, have now led to the introduction of ESP in school education in some places. This means that the science teacher and the teacher of English in a given school are now collaborators in a sense which has never previously existed.

The extreme case of such collaboration is found in those countries (e.g Zambia, Singapore) where the teaching of English and of science at school are being integrated. The Singapore Primary Pilot Project, for example, following government policy to promote bilingualism in Chinese (or Malay or Tamil) and English, divided the primary school curriculum into three blocks of subjects:
  (1) English, Mathematics and general science (occupying 43% of class time);
  (2) education for living, combining history, geography, civics (occupying 43% of class time);
  (3) Music, physical education, etc. (occupying 14% of class time).

The intention is that block (1) should be taught in English, block (2) in the mother tongue, and block (3) in either, depending on the preference of the school. This means that mathematics and science are taught in English and English is to be taught through mathematics and science, using a fully integrated syllabus.

Fortuitous collaboration elsewhere has not always been as fruitful as in places where it has been deliberately organized. Indeed, in many places teachers of science and of English have grounds for mutual suspicion. Teachers of English often find that teachers of science not only underestimate the very real difficulties of teaching a foreign language but also criticize unfairly when their pupils in science display an inadequate command of English. In fact, in many countries the teaching of foreign languages is organized in ways that tend to minimize chances of success and maximize chances of failure: e.g. objectives are often ill-defined; teaching is thinly spread; courses are often too long (10 years for a fairly simple syllabus is a recipe for boredom and failure); teachers may possess insufficient command of the language they are teaching; pupils and their parents may in some countries place a low value on learning English; and so forth. Language teaching is often a difficult, unglamorous, ill-rewarding job, and teachers of English in such conditions find it hard to accept criticism of the standards they achieve, even when these criticisms are justified.

Teachers of science overseas, for their part, sometimes have grounds for complaint that the teachers of English pass on to their pupils attitudes antagonistic towards science, thereby causing many learners who might otherwise elect to study science subjects to stay within the humanities, and creating difficulties of morale with some of those who do study science. The origins of this lie within certain schools of thought in English literature which seek to elevate literary criticism to pre-eminence as the arbiter of morals and ethics and which hold dogmatic and ill-justified views on the responsibility of science for various evils afflicting mankind. Of course it is a valuable part of education that children and students should consider the social consequences of developments in technology and science. But these discussions should be conducted from the standpoint that the teacher of science and the teacher of English are partners in education, with shared responsibility for helping their pupils towards wisdom. To achieve this, teachers must first understand each other's profession and arrive not necessarily at agreement, but at least at mutual acceptance and toleration.

Fortunately, the institutionalization of contact and collaboration between science educators and the English teachers (at the level of applied linguistics) has begun, not least as a result of two major international conferences and their published proceedings.

In August 1969 the Fifth Rehovot Conference on Science and Education in Developing Countries was held in Israel. It devoted a session and discussion time to language problems in science education (Strevens, 1971). Partly as a result of contacts made at that time and continued in subsequent years, a special UNESCO symposium was held in Nairobi in 1974, on Interactions Between Linguistics and Mathematical Education. The report of the symposium contains many illuminating and valuable papers: it is likely to give rise to further publications in due course.

From the other end of the spectrum, the teaching of English for science and technology is now established as an important area of English teaching, and one which demands the creation of continuous links between those who teach English and those who teach science.

IV

It seems, then, that the solution to the special problems of learning science through a foreign language is dependent upon achieving the maximum fit between five parameters: (i) the nature of *the science* being taught, which determines the language content and thus sets the limits of the language learning task; (ii) *the language situation,* which largely determines the extent and type of language difficulties; (iii) *the sociolinguistic and cultural situation,* which determines the extent of unfamiliarity of scientific concepts to the learner and their manifestation in his language; (iv) *the stage of national educational development,* which determines both how easy or difficult it may be for a particular scheme of science education to be put into effect and also what general standards of ability in English may be expected in the teaching profession; and (v) *the pedagogical situation,* which, on the one hand, determines the shape of the languge problems in the science classroom and on the other, determines the nature of the professional resources in English teaching (and teacher training) that may be called upon for assistance.

Teachers of English would not wish to exaggerate the assistance they can give. The teaching of science is the responsibility of science teachers, and many of them achieve their results without major language problems, or they overcome these by their own resources. Nevertheless, there are two ways in which either the teachers of English themselves or more likely the echelon of applied lingusitics can be of help to the science teacher. The first arises when the science teacher identifies language problems of a type or magnitude that go beyond his own resources; the second arises when the science teacher finds that his own students of science are also students of English for science or technology; and this is an area of professional concern where much mutual enlightenment can be hoped for in the future.

Bibliography

Allen, J. P. B. and Corder, S. P. (eds.) (1974) *The Edinburgh Course in Applied Linguistics,* 4 vols., Oxford University Press, London.

Altman, H. B. (1979) Foreign language teaching: focus on the learner, in Altman and James (1980).

Altman, H. B. and James, C. V. (eds.) (1980) *Foreign Language Learning: Meeting Communicative Needs,* Pergamon Press, Oxford.

Altman, H. B. and Politzer, R. L. (eds.) (1977) *Individualising Foreign Language Instruction,* Newbury House, Rowley, Mass.

Barber, C. L. (1962) Some measurable characteristics of modern scientific prose, *Contributions to English syntax and philology,* Stockholm.

Beeby, C. E. (1966) *The Quality of Education in Developing Countries,* Harvard University Press.

Bernstein, B. (1967) *Elaborated and restricted codes,* in S. Lieberson (ed.), *Explorations in Sociolinguistics,* Bloomington, Indiana.

Bickerton, D. (1975) *Dynamics of a Creole System,* Cambridge University Press, London.

Bloomfield, L. (1933) *Language.* Holt, New York.

Bowen, D.A. (1976) in *Workpapers in Teaching English as a Second Language,* University of California, Los Angeles.

Breen, M. and Candlin, C. (1980a) *The Communicative Curriculum in Language Teaching,* Longman, London.

Breen, M. and Candlin, C. (1980b) The essentials of a communicative curriculum in language teaching, *Applied Linguistics,* Vol. 1, No. 2.

Brumfit, C. J. (1980) *Problems and Principles in English Teaching,* Pergamon Press, Oxford.

Brumfit, C. J. and Johnson, K. (eds.) (1980) *The Communicative Approach to Language Teaching,* Oxford University Press, Oxford.

Bullock, A. (1975) *A Language for Life,* HMSO, London.

Bung, K. (1973) *The Specification of Objectives in a Language-learning System for Adults.* Council of Europe CCC/EES (73) 16, Strasbourg. Republished 1980, Pergamon Press, Oxford.

Burt, M. K., Dulay, H. C., and Finocchiaro, M. (eds.) (1977) *Viewpoints on English as a Second Language,* Regents, New York.

Candlin, C. N. (ed.) (1975) *The Communicative Teaching of English,* Longman, London.

Candlin, C. N. (1976) Communicative language teaching and the debt to pragmatics, in Rameh, C. (ed.), *27th Round Table on Languages and Linguistics,* monograph Series, University Press, Georgetown.

Candlin, C. N. (1979) Discoursal patterning and the equalising of interpretive opportunity, in Smith, L. (ed.), *English for Cross-Cultural Communication,* East-West Center, Hawaii.

Candlin, C. N., Bruton, C. J., and Leather, J. L. (1974) *Doctor-Patient Communications Skills,* Working Papers 1-4, Lancaster University (mimeographed).

Candlin, C. N., Bruton, C. J., and Leather, J. L., (1976a) Doctors in casualty: applying communicative competence to components of specialist course design, *IRAL* Vol. XIV, No. 3.

Candlin, C. N., Bruton, C. J., and Leather, J. L., (1976b) Doctor speech functions in casualty consultations, in Nickel, G., (ed.), *Proc. IV AILA Congress 1975,* Hochschulverlag, Stuttgart.

Chomsky, N. (1965) *Aspects of the Theory of Syntax,* MIT Press, Harvard.

Cooper, R. L. (1979) Language planning, language spread, and language change, in *30th Round Table on Languages and Linguistics,* Monograph Series, University Press, Georgetown.

Corder, S. P. (1973) *Introducing Applied Linguistics,* Penguin, Harmondsworth.

Corder, S. P. (1974) The significance of learners' errors, *IRAL* Vol. V, No. 4. Reprinted in Richards, 1974.

Corder, S. P. (1975) Error analysis, interlanguage and second language acquisition, *Language Teaching and Linguistics: Abstracts,* Vol. 8, No. 4.

Coste, D. *et al.* (1976) *Un Niveau-Seuil,* Council of Europe, Strasbourg.

Cowan, J. R. (ed.) (1977) Language for special purposes, special issue of *Studies in Language Learning,* Vol. 2, No. 1, Fall 1977. University of Illinois, Urbana-Champaign.

Currie, W. B., Sturtridge, G., and Allwright, J. (1972) A technique of teaching medical English, in *Proceedings of the International Congress on Applied Linguistics,* Vol. 3, Groosverlag, Heidelberg.

Diller, K. C. (1971) *Generative Grammar, Structural Lingusitics, and Language Teaching,* Newbury House, Rowley.

Donovan, P. (for ELTDU) (1978) *Basic English for Science,* Teacher's Book; Student's Book, Oxford University Press, Oxford.

Ewer, J. R. and Hughes-Davies, E. (1970) Further notes on developing an ELT programme for students of science and technology (mimeographed), Santiago, Chile.

Ewer, J. R. and Latorre, G., (1967) Preparing an English course for students of science, *English Language Teaching, Vol. XXI, No. 3.*

Fathman, A. K., (1976) Variables affecting the successful learning of English as a second language, *TESOL Quart.,* Vol. 10, No. 4.

Fillmore, C. J. (1968) The case for case, in Bach, E. and Harms, R. T. (eds.) *Universals in Lingusitic Theory,* Holt, Rinehart and Winston, New York.

Firth, J. R. (1957a) *Papers in Linguistics 1934-1951,* Blackwell, Oxford.

Firth, J. R. (1957b) *Studies in Lingusitic Analysis,* Blackwell, Oxford.

Fishman, J. A., Cooper, R. L. and Conrad, A. W., (1977) *The spread of English: The Sociology of English as an Additional Language,* Newbury House, Rowley, Mass.

Fried, V. (ed.) (1972) *The Prague School of Linguistics and Language Teaching,* Oxford University Press, London.

Fries, C. C. (1945) *Teaching and Learning English as a Foreign Language,* University of Michigan Press, Ann Arbor.

Gay, J. and Cole, M. (1967) *The New Mathematics and an Old Culture,* Holt, Rinehart & Winston, New York.

Giles, H. and Powesland, P. (1975) *Speech Style and Social Evaluation,* Academic Press, London.

Gingras, R. (ed.) (1979) *Second Language Acquisition and Foreign Language Teaching,* Center for Applied Lingusitics, Washington DC.

Halliday, M. A. K. (1970) *A Course in Spoken English: Intonation,* Oxford University Press, London.

Halliday, M. A. K. (1973) *Explorations in the Functions of Language,* Edward Arnold, London.

Halliday, M. A. K. (1975) *Learning how to mean: Explorations in the Development of Language,* Edward Arnold, London.

Halliday, M. A. K. (1978) *Languages as Social Semiotic: The Social Interpretation of Language and Meaning,* Edward Arnold, London.

Halliday, M. A. K. and Hasan R. (1976) *Cohesion in English,* Longman, London.

Hawkey, R. A. (ed.) (1978) *English for Specific Purposes,* British Council English Teaching Information Centre, London.

Hawkey, R. A. (1979) Syllabus design for specific purposes, in Altman and James (1980).

Hill, A. A. (1958) *Introduction to Linguistic Structures,* Harcourt, Brace, New York.

Holden, S. (ed.) (1977) *English for Specific Purposes,* Modern English Publications, London.

Holec, H. (1978) *Autonomie et Apprentissage des Langues,* Council of Europe, Strasbourg.

Hornby, A. A. (1948-1980) *Oxford Advanced Learner's Dictionary of Current English,* Oxford University.

Hornby, A. A. (1955) *Guide to Patterns and Usage in English,* Oxford University Press, London.

Hornby, A. S. (1966) *The Teaching of Structural Words and Sentence Patterns* (3 books), Oxford University Press, London.

Hoy, P. (ed.) (1977) *The Early Teaching of Foreign Languages,* Nuffield Foundation, London.

Huddleston, R. D. (1971) *The Sentence in Written English,* Cambridge University Press, Cambridge.

Jespersen, O. (1904) *How to Teach a Foreign Language,* Allen & Unwin, London. Reprinted 1947.

Johnson, K. (1976) The production of functional materials and their integration within existing language-teaching programmes, *ELT Documents,* No. 2, British Council, London.

Jones, D. (1960) *An Outline of English Phonetics,* Heffer, Cambridge

Jones, K. (1975) The role of discourse analysis in devising undergraduate reading programmes in English for science and technology (unpublished paper, quoted in Candlin (1979)).

Kachru, B. B. (1965) The *Indianness* in Indian English, *Word,* Vol. 21.

Kachru, B. B. (1975) Lexical innovations in South Asian English, *International Journal of the Sociology of Language,* Vol. 4.

Kachru, B. B. (1976a) Indian English: a sociolinguistic profile of a transplanted language, *Studies in Language Learning,* Vol. I, No. 2, University of Illinois.

Kachru, B. B. (1976b) Models of English for the Third World: white man's linguistic burden or language pragmatics? *TESOL Quart.* Vol. 10, No. 2.

Kachru, B. B. (1976c) The New Englishes and old models (mimeographed), University of Illinois.

Kachru, B. B. (1980a) The pragmatics of non-native varieties of English, in Smith, L. (1979).

Kachru, B. B. (1980b) Models for New Englishes (mimeographed) University of Illinois.

Kennedy, C. (ed) (1978?—n.d.) ESP, special issues of *MALS Journal* (mimeographed), University of Birmingham.

Lackstrom, J., Selinker, L. and Trimble, L. (1972) Technical rhetorical principles and grammatical choice, in *Proceedings of the International Congress on Applied Linguistics.* Vol. 3. Groosverlag, Heidelberg.

Lado, R. (1964) *Language Teaching: A Scientific Approach,* McGraw-Hill, New York.

Mackey, W. F. (1965) *Language Teaching Analysis,* Longman, London.

Mackin, R. (1970) *A Course in Spoken English: Texts, Drills and Exercises,* Oxford University Press, London.

Marckwardt, A. H. (1958) *American English,* Oxford University Press, New York.

Morris, R. W. (ed.) (1974) *Interactions Between Linguistics and Mathematical Education,* UNESCO, Nairobi.

Morrow, K. and Johnson, K. (1976) Communicate: the English of social interaction (mimeographed), University of Reading.

Munby, J. (1978) *Communicative Syllabus Design,* Cambridge University Press, Cambridge.

Oller, J. W. and Richards, J. C. (eds.) (1973) *Focus on the Learner: Pragmatic Perspectives for the Language Teacher,* Newbury House, Rowley, Mass.

Owens, R. J. (1960) *Words and Structures in Science and Mathematics,* Teacher Training College, Singapore.

Palmer, H. E. (1920) *The Principles of Language Study,* Oxford University Press, London. Reprinted 1964.

Paulston, C. B. and Bruder, M. N. (1976) *Teaching English as a Second Language: Techniques and Procedures,* Winthrop, New York.

Prator, C. P. (1968) The British Heresy in TESL, in Fishman, J. *et al.* (eds.), *Language Problems in Developing Nations,* Wiley, New York.

Quirk, R. (1972) *The English Language and Images of Matter,* Oxford University Press, London.

Quirk, R. (1978) On the grammar of 'Nuclear English', in Smith (1980).

Quirk, R., Greenberg, S., Leech, G., and Svartvik J. (1972) *A Grammar of Contemporary English,* Longman, London.

Richards, J. C. (ed.) (1974) *Error Analysis: Perspectives on Second Language Acquisition,* Longman, London.

Richards, J. C. (1979) *Understanding Second and Foreign Language Learning: A Survey of Issues and Approaches,* Newbury House, Rowley.

Richards, J. C. (1979) Variation in Singapore English, in Crewe, W. (ed.) *The English Language in Singapore,* Eastern Universities Press, Singapore.

Richterich, R. and Chancerel, J.-L. (1977) *Identifying the Needs of Adults Learning a Foreign Language,* Council of Europe, Strasbourg; Pergamon Press, Oxford.

Rivers, W. M. (1972) *Speaking in Many Tongues: Essays in Foreign-language Teaching,* Newbury House, Rowley, Mass.

Rivers, W. M. and Temperley, M. S. (1978) *A Practical Guide to the Teaching of English as a Second or Foreign Language.*

Roberts, J. T. (1975) La Session Libre, *AVLA Jl,* Vol. 13, No. 1.

Roberts, P. (1964) *English Syntax,* Harcourt, Brace, & World, New York.

Roe, P. (1978) The notion of difficulty in scientific text (unpublished PhD thesis), University of Birmingham.

Roulet, E. (1976) *Un Niveau-Seuil,* Council of Europe, Strasbourg.

Rutherford, W. E. (1974) *Modern English,* Harcourt, Brace & World, New York.

Savignon, S. J. (1972) *Communicative Competence: An Experiment in Foreign-language Teaching,* Center for Curriculum Development, Philadelphia.

Schumann, J. M. (1979) Affective and social factors in second language learning, in Gingras (1979).

Selinker, L. (1972) Interlanguage, *IRAL,* Vol. X, No. 3. Reprinted in Richards (1974).

Selinker, L., Todd, R. M., and Trimble, L. (1976) Presuppositional rhetorical information in ESL discourse, *TESOL Quart.,* Vol. 10, No. 3.

Shaw, A. M. (1975) Approaches to a communicative syllabus in foreign language curriculum development (unpublished PhD thesis), University of Essex.

Shaw, W. (1980) A survey of uses of English in India and South-East Asia, in Smith (1980).

Sinclair, J. McH. (1972) *A Course in Spoken English: Grammar,* Oxford University Press, London.

Sinclair, J. McH. and Coulthard, R. M. (1975) *Towards an Analysis of Discourse,* Oxford University Press, London.

Skinner, B. F. (1957) *Verbal Behaviour,* Appleton-Century-Crofts, New York.

Smith, L. E. (ed.) (1980) *English for Cross-cultural Communication,* Macmillan, New York and London.

Spencer, J. W. (1963) *Language in Africa,* Cambridge University Press, London.

Spolsky, B. (1978) *Educational Linguistics: An Introduction,* Newbury House, Rowley, Mass.

Strevens, P. (1971) Alternatives to Daffodils—or scientist thou never wert, in *CILT Reports and Papers,* No. 7, Centre for Information on Language Teaching, London.

Strevens, P. (1972) *British and American English,* Collier-Macmillan, London.

Strevens, P. (1973) Technical, technological and scientific English, *English Language Teaching,* Vol. 27, No. 3.

Strevens, P. (1976) Problems of learning and teaching science through a foreign language, *Studies in Science Education,* Vol. 3, University of Leeds.

Strevens, P. (1977a) Causes of failure and conditions for success in the learning and teaching of languages, in Brown, H. D., Yorio, C. A. and Crymes, R. H. (eds.), *On TESOL '77,* TESOL, Washington, DC.

Strevens, P. (1977b) English for special purposes: an analysis and a survey, in Cowan (1977).

Strevens, P. (1978a) *New Orientations in the Teaching of English,* Oxford University Press, Oxford.

Strevens, P. (1978b) English as an international language: when is a local form of English a suitable target for ELT purposes? in *English as an International Language,* British Council English Teaching Information Centre, London.

Strevens, P. (1978c) Special-purpose language teaching: a perspective, in Kinsella, V. (ed.), *Language Teaching and Linguistics: Surveys,* Centre for Information on Language Teaching and Research, London.

Strevens, P. (1978d) English for International and Intranational Purposes: a shift in linguistic perspectives, *Indian Journal of Applied Linguistics,* Vol. IV, No. 1.

Strevens, P. (1979) Forms of English: an analysis of the variables, in Smith (1979).

Sweet, H. (1899) *The Practical Study of Languages: a Guide for Teachers and Learners,* Oxford University Press, London. Reprinted 1964.

Trager, G. L. and Smith, H. L. (1951) *Outline of English Structure.* *Studies in Linguistics* Occasional Papers No. 1. Norman, Oklahama.

Trim, J. L. (1974) A unit/credit scheme for adult language learning, in Perren, G. (ed.) *CILT Reports and Papers,* No. 11, Centre for Information on Language Teaching, London.

Trim J. L. (1978) *Some Possible Lines of Development of an Overall Structure for a European Unit/Credit Scheme for Foreign Language Learning by Adults.* Strasbourg. Council of Europe.

Trim, J. L. M., Richterich, R., Van Ek, J.A. and Wilkins, D. A. (1980) *Systems Development in Adult Language Learning,* Pergamon Press, Oxford.

Trimble, L. (1977) An approach to reading scientific and technical English, *Linguas Para Objectivos Específicos,* Vol. 4, Autonomous University, Mexico City.

Trimble, M. T., Trimble, L., and Drobnic, K. (eds.) (1978) *English for Specific Purposes: Science and Technology,* Oregon State University, English Language Institute, Seattle.

Tongue, R. K. (1974) *The English of Singapore and Malaysia,* Eastern Universities Press, Singapore.

Trudgill, P. (1974) *The Social Differentiation of English in Norwich,* Cambridge University Presss, Cambridge.

Tucker, G. R. (1975) New directions in second language teaching, in Troike, R. C. and Modiano, N. (eds.) *Proceedings of the First Inter-American Conference on Bi-lingual Education,* Center for Applied Linguistics, Arlington, Va.

Tucker, G. R. (1978) The implementation of language teaching programs, in Richards (1978).

UNESCO-CEDO-ICMI (1974) *Internactions between Linguistics and Mathematical Education,* UNESCO, Nairobi.

Van Ek, J. A. (1975) *The Threshold Level,* Council of Europe, Strasbourg. Republished 1980, Pergamon Press, Oxford.

Van Ek, J. A. (1976) *The Threshold Level for Modern Language Learning in Schools,* Longman, Harlow.

Van Ek, J. A. and Alexander L. G. (1977) *Waystage,* Council of Europe, Strasbourg, Republished Pergamon Press, Oxford, 1980.

Webb, J. (1975) Reflections on practical experience in designing and mounting ESP courses, *ARELS Jl*, Vol. 2, No. 1, Association of Recognised English Language Schools, London.

White, R. V. (1975) The language learner and the syllabus, *RELC Jl*, Vol. 6, No. 1, Regional English Language Centre, Singapore.

Widdowson, H. G. (1968) The teaching of English through science, in Dakin, J., Tiffen, B., and Widdowson, H. G., (eds.) *Language in Education*, Oxford University Press, London.

Widdowson, H. G. (1975) *Stylistics and the Teaching of Literature*, Longman, Harlow.

Widdowson, H. G. (1978) *Teaching Language as Communication*, Oxford University Press, Oxford.

Widdowson, H. G. (1979) *Explorations in Applied Linguistics*, Oxford University Press, Oxford.

Wilkins, D. A. (1973) The linguistic and situational content of the common core in a unit/credit system, in Trim, J. L., Richterich, R., Van Ek, J. A., and Wilkins, D. A., (eds.), *Systems Development in Adult Language Learning*, Pergamon Press, Oxford. 1980.

Wilkins, D. A. (1976) *Notional Syllabuses*, Oxford University Press, London.

Zandvoort, R. W. (1975) *A Handbook of English Grammar*, Longmans, London.

Index

Accents of English 66-71
  see also Standard English; Dialects
      of English
Acronyms
  EFL, ESL, ELT, TEFL, TESL,
      TESOL, TESOD, TESOLD,
      ESP, EST, EOP, EAP 31-33
  L1/L2 (primary language/secondary
      language) 71
  FL/SL (foreign language/second lan-
      guage) 72
Adult learners 8
Allwright, J. 111, 153
Altman, H.A. 113, 151
Applied linguistics 9, 77, 105, 112, 115
Approach
  as an element in a theory of lan-
      guage teaching/learning 8, 13
  communicative 114
  see also Notions, notional syllabuses;
      Syllabus
Audiolingual method 13, 49

Beeby, C. 143, 151
Black English 32, 70, 75
Bloomfield, L. 47, 151
  Bloomfieldian linguistics 49, 50
  see also Structural linguistics
Bruton, J. 114, 152
Bung, K. 114, 151

Candlin, C. 114, 115, 152
Chancerel, J-L. 114, 156
Chomsky, N. 47, 50, 152
Cognitive code theory 50
Corder, S. P. 83, 152
Coulthard, M. 115, 157
Council of Europe
  languages project 115, 116-18
  systems approach 114

Cowan, J. R. 113, 152
Currie, W. B. 111, 153

Dialects of English 66-71
  defining localized forms (LFEs, q.v.)
      66
  linked with accents 66-67
  Standard English 67-71
Diller, K. 118n, 153
Direct method 13, 48, 118
Donovan, P. 119, 153

Educator, teacher as 4
English for specific purposes (ESP)
      35, 105-21, 147
  bibliographies 121
  definition 108-9
  claims made for 119
  pre-requisites for success 120
English language
  localized forms (LFEs) 61-78
  spread of 61-78
  number of users 62, 84
  international and intranational pur-
      poses for (INTER/INTRA)
      79-90, 91-101
  global family of 85-86
  nature of 'scientific English' 109,
      122-135, 138
Evaluation 37

Failure in language learning, causes of
      18-28
Fillmore, C. 116, 153
Firth, J. R. 51, 153
  neo-Firthian linguistics 115
Fishman, J. 105, 106, 153
Foreign languages (not specifically
      English) 5-6
Fries, C. C. 47, 118n, 153

Grammar-translation method   48
Greenbaum, S.   52, 155

Halliday, M. A. K.   51-52, 115, 116, 145, 153
Hawkey, R.   113, 154
Hill, A. A.   47, 49, 154
Holden, S.   113, 154
Hornby, A. S.   43-58, 118n

Immigrants, teaching English to   32
Instructor, teacher as   4
Intensity of teaching/learning   23, 26

James, C. V.   113, 151
Jespersen, O.   47, 52, 118n, 154
Johnson, K.   118, 154, 155
Jones, D.   48, 154

Kachru, B. B.   89, 95, 105, 154
Kennedy, C.   112, 154

Lado, R.   47, 118n, 155
Learner
  adult   8
  changed expectations   8
  special linguistic abilities   10
  needs-analysis   108, 109
Learning of language
  achievement in   18-28
  failure and success in   18-28
Leather, J. L.   114, 152
Leech, J.   52, 155
Linguistics
  place of, in language teaching   12, 44-45, 77
  chronology   47-48
  schools of thought
    Bloomfieldian   49, 50
    Chomskyan   47, 50
    Hallidayan   51-52
    neo-Firthian   115
    systemic   115
    transformational-generative   47, 50

Literature
  study of   6
  English the vehicle for, as secondary language   73, 74
Localized Forms of English (LFEs)   61-78

Mackey, W. F.   33, 155
Mackin, R.   52n, 118n, 155
Marckwardt, A.   48, 118n, 155
Materials   14, 24, 49, 118-19
Methodology   6, 14, 35, 49, 120-121
Mixed-ability, classes of   6-7, 49
Morris, R. W.   138
Morrow, K.   118, 155
Mother-tongue
  teaching of   7
  acquisition of   9
Motivation   39n
  avoidance of the term   39n
  highly-motivated students   49
  in ESP   119
  unmotivated students   49
Munby, J.   114, 118, 155

Needs-analysis of learner, in ESP   108-9, 114
Notions, notional syllabuses   115-17
  see also Syllabus

Palmer, H. E.   47, 52, 118n, 155
Phonetics   48
Prague School of linguistics and language teaching   51
Prator, C.   92, 155
Process of language learning/teaching   3-5
Profession of language teaching   3-16, 18-42
Professionalism in teaching   3-17, 23, 27
  pedagogical professionalism of Britain contrasted with disciplinary professionalism of U. S.   56

Quirk, R.   47, 52, 53, 64, 94-95, 155

Richterich, R.   114, 156
Roberts, P.   47, 156
Rutherford, W.   47, 118n, 156

Selinker, L.   83, 156
Shaw, A. M.   118, 156
Sinclair, J. McH.   47, 51-52, 114, 157
Skinner, B. F.   48, 49, 157
Smith, H. L. (Trager and)   48, 158
Smith, Larry E.   93, 104, 157
Standard English   67-71
    see also Dialects; Accents
Structural linguistics   56
Sturtridge, G.   111, 153
Success in language learning
    conditions for   18-28
    in ESP   119
Svartvik, J.   52, 155
Sweet, Henry   47, 52, 118n, 158
Syllabus   13, 26, 35-37
    notional, functional, communicative
        36-37, 108, 114-18
    in ESP   108
    design of   118
    for teaching science in English   137
    linguistic   118
    situational   118

Taiwo, C.   141
Teacher, professional career develop-
    ment of   4-5
Teacher, training of   13, 16, 24, 38, 43,
    76, 77, 150
Teaching as 'management of learning'
    3
Teaching, intensity of   15
Trager, G. L.   48, 158
Transformational-generative grammar
    (TG)   46-47, 50
Trim, J. L.   114, 117, 158

Van Ek, J.   114, 117, 158
Variables
    in teaching   29-42, 149
    in learning   82-83

Widdowson, H. G.   114, 159
White, R. V.   123, 159
Wilkins, D.A.   114, 115, 117, 159

Zandvoort, R. W.   51, 159